SPOOKY Maine

Tales of Hauntings, Strange Happenings, and Other Local Lore

RETOLD BY S. E. SCHLOSSER

ILLUSTRATED BY PAUL G. HOFFMAN

Globe Pequot

ESSEX, CONNECTICUT

Globe Pequot

An imprint of The Globe Pequot Publishing Group, Inc.
64 South Main Street
Essex, CT 06426
www.globepequot.com

Illustrations by Paul G. Hoffman

British Library Cataloguing in Publication Information available

Library of Congress Cataloging-in-Publication Data

Names: Schlosser, S. E. author | Hoffman, Paul G. illustrator
Title: Spooky Maine : tales of hauntings, strange happenings, and other local lore / retold by S. E. Schlosser ; illustrated by Paul G. Hoffman.
Description: Essex, Connecticut : Globe Pequot, [2026] | Includes bibliographical references. | Summary: "Maine traditions are kept alive in these expert retellings by master storyteller S. E. Schlosser and through artist Paul G. Hoffman's evocative illustrations."— Provided by publisher.
Identifiers: LCCN 2025051078 (print) | LCCN 2025051079 (ebook) | ISBN 9781493089956 paperback | ISBN 9781493089963 epub
Subjects: LCSH: Haunted places—Maine | Ghosts—Maine | Tales—Maine | Legends—Maine | Maine—History
Classification: LCC BF1472.U6 S299 2026 (print) | LCC BF1472.U6 (ebook)
LC record available at https://lccn.loc.gov/2025051078
LC ebook record available at https://lccn.loc.gov/2025051079

For my family: David, Dena, Tim, Arlene, Hannah, Seth, Theo, Rory, Emma, Nathan, Ben, Jess, Deb, Gabe, Clare, Jack, Chris, Karen, Davey, and Aunt Mil.

For Aunt Lynetta, Uncle John, Dan, Marisol, Anne, Nathan, Nathaniel, Melinda, Mary Elizabeth, and Hannah.

For Meredith Dias, Paul Hoffman, and all the wonderful folks at Globe Pequot Press, with my thanks.

For the staff of Lubec Memorial Library. Thanks for your help!

In memory of Kirsten Bray.

Contents

MAP viii

INTRODUCTION xi

PART ONE: GHOST STORIES 1

1 *The Leaky Kettle* 3
MOUNT DESERT ISLAND

2 *The Watcher* 13
APPLEDORE

3 *The Special* 19
JACKMAN

4 *The Girl in the Graveyard* 25
BRUNSWICK

5 *Weird Helmsman* 31
SCHOONER HEAD, ACADIA NATIONAL PARK

6 *Hope Chest* 37
BANGOR

7 *Do You Need a Shave?* 45
EASTPORT

8 *The Photograph* 53
LONG LAKE

9 *Death Light* 63
CAPE ELIZABETH

10 *A Strange Encounter* 69
MACHIASPORT

11 *The Sarah* 77
FREEPORT

12 *Playing Piano* 87
PHIPPSBURG

13 *Turning the Tables* 93
ANDROSCOGGIN COUNTY

PART TWO: POWERS OF DARKNESS AND LIGHT 103

14 *The Witch Bridle* 105
KITTERY

15 *Specter Moose* 111
SHERMAN

16 *La Chasse Galerie* 119
ST. JOHN VALLEY

17 *Nicodemus* 127
SOMERSET COUNTY

18 *The Other List* 137
PORTLAND

19 *Dance with the Devil* 147
LUBEC

20 *The Wizard* 153
HALLOWELL

21 *The Cursed Tomb* 159
BUCKSPORT

22 *The Sandman* 165
YORK HARBOR

23 *The Sailor's Dream* 171
KENNEBUNKPORT

24 *Ten Dollars* 181
FORT KENT

25 *Logging* 187
BUCKFIELD

RESOURCES 197
ABOUT THE AUTHOR 205
ABOUT THE ILLUSTRATOR 205

SPOOKY SITES . . .

1. Mount Desert Island
2. Appledore
3. Jackman
4. Brunswick
5. Schooner Head, Overlook, Acadia National Park
6. Bangor
7. Eastport
8. Long Lake
9. Cape Elizabeth
10. Machiasport
11. Freeport
12. Phippsburg
13. Androscoggin County
14. Kittery
15. Sherman
16. St. John Valley
17. Somerset County
18. Portland
19. Lubec
20. Hallowell
21. Bucksport
22. York Harbor
23. Kennebunkport
24. Fort Kent
25. Buckfield

AND WHERE TO FIND THEM

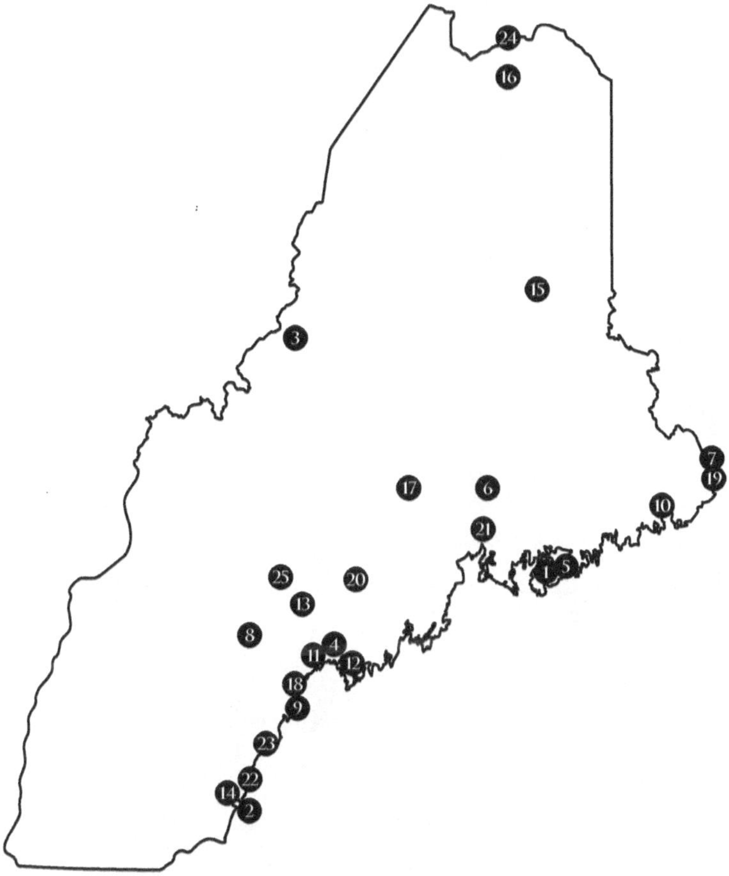

Introduction

I got up at the crack of dawn to avoid the Labor Day crowds. The drive to Maine was long, but I managed to avoid the worst of the traffic jams with the aid of vanilla coffee and a good audiobook. I made it to Kittery—once home of old Betty Booker (The Witch Bridle) by 1:00 p.m., before the hotel room was ready. Taking advantage of the delay, I drove to the York Historical Society to visit the museum and attached buildings. Somewhere deep in the archives, there was a haunted Bible that once belonged to Old Trickey, the Sandman. According to legend, whenever someone opened the book, it would immediately slam shut of its own accord.

When I arrived at my destination, I was disappointed to learn the Trickey Bible was no longer on display in the upstairs gallery, but there were many other interesting items from portraits of ships to old seamen's trunks (Hope Chest) that enticed me to linger in the exhibit hall.

Downstairs, I wandered into a low-ceiling tavern, originally from Wells, Maine. I was all over goose bumps as I gazed at the long gleaming table and the wide fireplace hearth. This place reminded me of a certain Down East tavern said to be haunted by a barber's ghost (Do You Need a Shave?). It felt as if I'd stepped back in time. Then a staff member hurried into the space to give me a tour, and the twenty-first century reasserted itself.

After bidding my guide farewell, I ventured across the street to the cemetery to see the grave of Mary, who was reputed to be a white witch back in the colonial period. Many gifts and offerings had been left on the flat slab behind her headstone. Folklore claimed that the slab was laid down to keep her body from rising from the grave, but in reality, it was designed to keep wild animals from digging her up, a precaution taken by her grieving husband who moved away from the area after she perished. Mary's spirit is said to haunt the cemetery and surrounding area.

My next destination was the Old York Gaol. As soon as I set foot on the property, I felt multiple layers in the atmosphere. A shiver ran through my arms and legs as the sixth sense I'd inherited from my Pennsylvania Dutch grandfather kicked in. Haunted jail house? Check.

Taking a calming breath, I walked into the front yard of the old gaol, where I met a lovely couple who volunteered to take my photo with the red-painted building. It was a thoughtful gesture, and I thanked them warmly before continuing downhill to examine the cannon and stocks on display.

Next, I followed a stone pathway to the side entrance and showed my ticket to the guide. She was halfway through a group tour, so I opted to wander around the public rooms by myself, looking at the exhibits and reading the documentation before heading over to the jail section. As I stepped into the first room, I overheard the guide describing several jailhouse incidents, including the story of a prisoner who grew so thin he escaped through a chimney hole.

When the tour moved on, I entered the jail cells through a low door and stopped abruptly. I did not like this place.

Not one bit. Shivering, I peered around the small cell. It had barred pass-through windows on two sides and a door leading to another room. Local lore claimed there was a ghost in the Old York Gaol, a woman named Patience who was convicted of murder and hanged for her crime. Her confession and message of repentance were displayed on one of the tattered old walls.

I moved into the second cell, which had another barred window that filtered daylight into the space. The quarters were tight, the ceiling was low, and the atmosphere was heavy. An unseen presence stirred restlessly as I entered the room, and I caught my breath sharply. This melancholy soul was so fractured and out-of-sorts that it couldn't communicate properly. The weight of its presence within the cell was unbearable. It wanted to be left alone, so I quickly exited the jail and then the building. I'd had enough for one day. I heaved a sigh of relief once I was off the grounds. That was . . . intense.

I drove back to the hotel to check in. Once I had settled into my room, I headed to the Kittery Trading Post in search of a light jacket to wear on my Monday boat tour. According to legend, a Death Light regularly appeared in Casco Bay just off Cape Elizabeth, signaling the fate of a murdered sailor. The boat would pass right over the location during the tour!

I ordered dinner at a local clam hut on the tidal stream and sat flicking lazily through the photos of Old York while I waited for my number to come up. I stopped abruptly when I reached the picture the couple had taken of me at the Old York Gaol and my mouth dropped open in shock. There I stood, smiling sweetly at the camera, and beside me floated a phantom, glowing eerily for the camera. We made a nice pair. *Hello ghost. What are you doing in my picture?*

I examined the streams of light pouring over my left side. They formed a luminous figure that was still in motion. The camera had captured the ghost midway through its manifestation. I'd known when I walked onto the grounds that the place was haunted, but to have such visual evidence gave me chills.

Flicking through a few more images, I found a second photo of the phantom from a different angle. I'd gone down the slope to get a panoramic view of the old gaol, and from that position the phantom could be seen floating a few feet above the ground. It had solidified into a column of light about halfway between my position and the red building. I gulped and put my phone away. When researching for this trip, I'd read a newspaper article about some Maine vacationers who'd captured a ghost on film in the 1920s (The Photograph). I never thought it would happen to me.

My order was called, and I went to get my tray from the window. Boy, was I glad to be away from that haunted spot! I'd sit right here at this picnic table and enjoy my fresh clams, ghost-free. Hard to believe this was only my first day in spooky Maine. Tomorrow's itinerary included a visit to Old Trickey's haunted beach, the Nubble lighthouse where the *Isadore* ghost ship had been sighted (The Sailor's Dream), and the International Cryptozoology Museum in Portland, which featured Bigfoot, the Casco Bay monster, and the Specter Moose. There was plenty of spookiness still ahead of me. But for now, I was going to eat some seafood.

Happy hauntings,
Sandy Schlosser

PART ONE

Ghost Stories

The Leaky Kettle

MOUNT DESERT ISLAND

I held the offending container up to my eye with a frown. Yes, the old kettle had sprung a leak. Tarnation. I was the third generation to use it, so I couldn't say it hadn't done well by us. But I prided myself on my thrift and had hoped to get a few more years out of the elderly kettle before time took its final toll.

I put the old kettle onto the kitchen table, filled a pot from the pump, and set it on the back burner of the wood stove to heat. Then I opened the window beside the sink, shivering as a cold breeze blew into my cozy haven.

"Teddy, when is Pots and Pans Man coming?" I called to my husband, who was outside chopping wood in anticipation of the weather. Storm clouds were massing, and we expected snow to fly later in the day.

"He should have been here by now," Ted called back, setting down the axe and pulling out his handkerchief to wipe his forehead. "He usually comes through in September."

I knew that, of course, but wanted my husband's confirmation. Pots and Pans Man was my third—or was it fourth?—cousin once removed. His branch of the family were

THE LEAKY KETTLE

very successful peddlers who traveled to many communities with supplies and fancies. He'd been coming around to all the family houses up and down the coast since I was a little girl, and we always gave him a bed for the night when he reached Bar Harbor.

"Did something happen to one of your pots, Sally?" Ted asked, coming to stand beside the open window.

"The old kettle has a leak," I said.

"I can go to town and get a new one once I finish stacking the wood," my husband offered.

"You know we buy all our kitchen goods from Pots and Pans Man," I said reproachfully. "He's kin."

"Yes, dear, but he isn't here," Ted said patiently. "And with winter settling in, he may not be here until spring. That's a long time to go without tea."

I frowned, tapping my fingers on the cold windowsill restlessly. "Do you think something happened to him?" I asked, lowering my voice. People were not always kind to peddlers. You heard stories.

"I hope not," Ted said, covering my chilly finger with his warm ones. "Frank is my favorite peddler-cousin-by-marriage. How about we make a deal? Let's wait until Christmas Eve to get a new kettle. If Pots and Pans hasn't arrived by then, I'll get you one for Christmas. Will that do?"

I thought about it for a moment, then nodded. "And I'll write to my sister Betty in Portland and see if she has heard anything about Frank."

"That's my girl," Ted said approvingly. He kissed me through the opening and went back to cutting wood. I shut the window and went back to check the pot on the stove. There would be tea with lunch, even if the kettle was broken.

Ted had refilled the indoor wood pile and set another stack of logs within easy reach of the back door by lunchtime. I roasted a small duck for our meal with fresh bread and drippings, which my husband devoured with enthusiasm. Then Ted bundled up and went to the barn to settle our livestock before the storm, while I put the duck bones with some herbs and root vegetables into a stock pot—courtesy of my cousin Frank—to make a broth. I stored the remaining leftovers in the cold cellar, though I could just as easily have left them on the back porch, since the outside temperature was below freezing.

Around 2:00 p.m. the first snowflakes fell from the sky. The wind whisked them playfully here and there, before settling them on the ground. The fall had been unusually mild, but it looked like this snowstorm would stick.

I paused for a moment to watch the snow, feeling as giddy as a youngster at the sight. And then I heard the jingle of a harness and a familiar clink-clank sound coming down our lane. Speak of the devil! If that wasn't the sound of the Pots and Pans Man's wagon, then I was a Christmas goose.

I pulled on a shawl and stepped into the yard as Ted came eagerly out of the barn. "Well wife, this is a fine coincidence," he called, heading toward the lane.

"I call it Providence," I retorted with a smile and a wave for the man navigating his team through the swirling snow and into our yard. The wagon was filled to the brim with pots and pans and kitchen utensils in every shape and size and material. Frank always stocked the best quality goods. He told me he had to sell the best or the most unusual in order to compete with the local merchants.

Ted pulled open the barn doors and signaled Frank to drive the wagon inside. When Frank put on the brake and swung out of the driver's seat, Ted shook his hand enthusiastically. "We nearly gave up on you, Cousin Pots and Pans," he said jovially. "You are very late!"

I stepped forward to give my cousin a peck on the cheek. He was pale and far too thin, almost skeletal. There were dark rings around his eyes, which had sunk deep into his skull. Lines edged his cheeks and mouth. I thought perhaps it was illness that had kept him so long from our door.

"I will get supper started while you settle the horses," I told Frank. "You can have the spare room for however long you are in the area." He thanked me, and I left the two men to care for the horses trotting through the rapidly accumulating snow to my warm kitchen.

Sometime later, I heard the men stomping snow off on the threshold, and opened the door to let them in. I glanced around the twilight yard and saw a familiar set of footprints in snow that was already several inches deep. The prints led from the barn to the house, and I recognized the pattern from Ted's worn work boots. That was odd, I thought suddenly. There was only one set of footprints, not two. Pots and Pans Man must have walked directly behind my husband, matching his stride exactly, to avoid making marks in the snow. But why bother? I shivered uncertainly.

"Shut the door, Sally love," Ted called as he hung up the coats. "You're letting in the cold."

I promptly forgot the small mystery, bustling inside to tend to our guest and hear the latest gossip from down the coast. Dinner was beans and brown bread, and Frank ate every last bite, which he needed, given his skeletal frame. If I turned my head to one side, I could almost see the lantern shining right through him. The effect made my skin crawl, so I returned my attention to the conversation.

"Ted tells me you need a new kettle," Cousin Pots and Pans said with a grin. "I told you that last year, but you wouldn't listen to me."

"I got another full year out of that kettle, thank you very much," I said primly.

The men laughed. "My wife is very thrifty, as you well know," Ted boasted.

"And she is a good cousin and a good customer," Frank said. "I thank you, cousin, for treating me so kindly all these years."

His smile was so sweet that I forgave his teasing and got him another cup of tea. I laid out an apple pie I'd been saving for dessert and sat in front of the fire talking about this and that until it was nine o'clock, time for bed. The snow had stopped by the time Ted showed my cousin to the spare room I'd made up for his visit, and we went to our own room to sleep.

I was up at first light and knocked on the door to the spare room to awaken Cousin Pots and Pans on my way downstairs. He didn't answer, which was strange. Frank was a light sleeper. He must be very tired from his long trip, I decided.

I went downstairs and got a brisk fire going in the stove. I had the coffee ready by the time Ted appeared in the kitchen.

"Where is Frank?" I asked, giving him a good morning kiss. "I knocked on his door earlier. He should be up."

"I knocked too, but he didn't answer," Ted replied. "Maybe he went out to feed the horses."

"Seems a might early for that," I said, hurrying to open the front door. The snow outside was pristine, not a mark to be seen, from man or creature. Ted's solo footprints from last night were filled in completely by the heavy snowfall.

"He must still be sleeping," Ted said, staring at the pristine snow gleaming in the dawn light. He ascended to the room at the top of the stairs and knocked loudly with both fists on the door, calling for Frank.

I followed him upstairs, my heart pounding with something akin to dread. Frank should have heard us knocking. He always answered right away. This silence was disturbing. I remembered his thin, almost skeletal face with the dark circles, the way the light seemed to shine through him when I glanced at him from the side. Had my cousin died during the night?

Ted received no answer and neither of us heard a sound from inside the room. My husband glanced questioningly at me, and I nodded. We respected Frank's privacy, but we needed to make sure he was all right. Since he was my kin, I stepped forward and turned the knob.

The door opened easily, and we both peered inside, expecting to see a still figure huddled under the bedclothes, his satchel on the chair where he'd placed it the night before. But the room was empty. The bed had not been slept in; the covers were smooth and carefully creased in the fancy way my mother taught me long ago. There was no satchel, the chamber pot was clean, and the wash basin was empty, though I'd given Frank a pitcher to take upstairs with him. Even the rag rug was clean and straight on the floor.

"He left?" Ted asked in amazement. "When? How? We would have seen his footprints in the snow."

He turned abruptly and ran down the stairs and out to the barn. I grabbed his coat and my shawl and followed him. As I hurried along, I noticed that my footprints never quite tracked with those of my husband, although we were going the same way. And I remembered, with a shiver, the single set of tracks in the snow when the men came into the house last evening.

Ted was standing in the barn, staring around in shock when I arrived. Horse and wagon were gone. No pots and pans, no horse droppings in the stalls, and the number of hay bales stacked against the wall was the same as it had been before Frank arrived.

My husband was pale and shaking when he turned to me. "I don't understand," he said, wringing his hands. "We opened a hay bale for Frank's horse and put him in the stall there. But the hay bale we used is stacked right there." He pointed with a trembling finger. "I remember it because it was the last bale with a reddish twist through the twine. The rest have a blue twist."

I drew in a deep breath, remembering how the lantern light seemed to shine through my cousin during the evening meal. "I think that something happened to Cousin Frank since his last visit," I said shakily. "I think his . . . his spirit came to say goodbye."

My big strong husband fainted.

We received a letter and a package from my sister in Portland a few days before Christmas. In the letter, Betty told us that

Cousin Frank, the Pots and Pans Man, had been robbed and murdered on a stretch of road between Freeport and Brunswick. His body was found in the bushes beside the road, along with a couple of pots and pans that had fallen from the wagon when the thieves drove away with his horse and wagon.

I read the final portion of the letter aloud: "Cousin Frank usually overwintered here in Portland. He left a present for you at my house last spring before he set out on his rounds. He said you would be wanting it later this year, and I should send it to you for Christmas. I told him he could give it to you when he visited Mount Desert Island, but he said it would be better if it came from me. I think he had a premonition that this summer would be his last trip."

Ted's eyes widened, and he urged me to open the package. I think we both knew what was inside. A moment later, the string was cut, the brown paper carefully folded back, and a gleaming kettle graced the center of the table. A small card written in Frank's hand said: "I thank you, cousin, for treating me so kindly all these years."

Rest in peace, Frank.

2

The Watcher

APPLEDORE

His health was failing that summer of 1826. He felt in his bones that he would not live much longer. His family, less resigned to fate than he, endeavored to bring him back to health by sending him to stay with a fisherman and his family on Star Island, which was part of the Isles of Shoals.

Summer slowly turned to autumn, and the solitude of the islands brought some solace to him. Watching the sun rise over the ocean, hearing the endless sound of the waves and the calling of birds, helped reconcile him to the immortality of the soul. It was autumn, and the mornings were remote and still. Strength slowly returned to his body, and he began to take short walks and even to sail a small boat around the islands.

One afternoon he rowed over to the island of Appledore for a stroll. The island was uninhabited and had been so ever since Maine taxes were assessed for the island township in the 1680s. The independent Shoalers, forty families strong, had decided they would rather live in New Hampshire than pay Maine taxes, so they had dismantled their homes and moved to Star Island. He chuckled to himself at the thought.

THE WATCHER

His wanderings took him out onto a long, low point backed by cliffs. He faced east, gazing across the sea. Suddenly he became aware of a woman standing but a few feet away. He had no notion from whence she came. He had heard no footsteps, seen no movement. She wore a dark cape, and her fair hair spilled over her shoulders. Her face was beautiful, but wan, and her blue eyes were fixed on the distance.

She must, he decided, be waiting for a fishing boat. Or perhaps she had a tryst here with a lover. He stood in silence, not wishing to disturb her reverie. At length, when no boat appeared in the distance, he said: "Do you see anything of him?"

She fixed melancholy blue eyes upon him and said: "He will come again." She turned away and walked out of sight around a jutting rock. Amazed, he took a few steps after her. But when he reached the rock, she had disappeared. His skin prickled with superstitious fear, for he could see no place where she could have hidden, or any reason for her to do so. He suddenly wished himself safe in his quarters on Star Island and beat a hasty retreat to his boat.

Back in his room, he thought perhaps the woman had been a dream, or an illusion brought about by his illness. She haunted his thoughts. The rest of the day, he gazed anxiously into the face of each of the women he saw on Star Island, hoping to see the woman he had met on Appledore. But there was none who resembled her. And when he described her to his hostess, she said she had never heard of her.

The next day the wind blew up a gale. He knew he should not go out in such weather, but he was haunted by the memory of the disappearing woman and was driven to return to Appledore to verify or deny her existence. Ignoring the warning of the fisherman, he sailed his small boat across the furious waves and found shelter in a cove on the leeward side of the island. He made his way to the point, but found it buried under a rolling sea. As he stood in the fierce wind, he heard a voice call over the waves: "He will come again." And then, as close as a breath, a low laugh sounded beside him. He whirled in terror, but there was no one there.

Obsessed with a desire to meet the woman again, he began visiting the island every day. As he stood on the point, often the golden-haired woman stood with him. His first terror gone, he noticed details about her now. The shells were not crushed beneath her feet. The wind never ruffled her hair. Her garments never rustled as she moved. And her attitude was one of deep stillness. Always, whether she spoke or stood in silence, he could sense her words: "He will come again."

He was shaky, jittery at all times now. The fisherman and his family were worried by his sudden nervous condition. But he could not seem to refrain from visiting the island with its ghost.

Then one evening as he stood on the western shore of Appledore, gazing at the sunset, the woman appeared beside him. As they watched the boats unfurl their white sails and depart for the night's fishing from the cove of Star Island, he turned to look at his companion. Just for a moment, in the light of sunset, the blue eyes softened and he could see the warmth and humanity that she had once possessed. The sight alarmed him as her presence never had. She had once been as human as he. What tragedy had tied her to this island, never to rest? The terror, held in check for many days, overwhelmed him and he ran away, vowing never to come again to Appledore or look upon its ghost.

Unbeknownst to him, the old fisherman, concerned for his health, had delayed his fishing that night in order to discover where his guest kept going. Upon his return from Appledore, the fisherman met him on the dock on Star Island. They walked together for a few moments in silence. Then the fisherman quietly told him the story of the Watcher.

Captain Teach, better known as Blackbeard, had once terrorized these waters. One of his comrades, a pirate called Captain Scot, had brought this fair lady to the Isles of Shoals. It was said that immense treasure had been buried by Blackbeard on Lunging Island, but Scot had buried his treasure separately and had made his lover swear that she would guard the treasure from all comers until he returned, be it until the Day of Judgment. Departing on a voyage to plunder, slash, and slay, Captain Scot was accidentally killed when a powder magazine blew up, leaving the woman alone to guard his treasure until the end of time.

"She is still there," said the fisherman. "Watching."

They both looked across the water at Appledore. The ghost's words rang once more through the man's mind: "He will come again." He wondered if she knew that her pirate lover was lost to her forever. He sighed, and his companion clapped a hand on his arm.

"Let's go home," said the fisherman. The man nodded. They turned away from the ghost of the past and headed for the warmth and light of home.

3

The Special

JACKMAN

I watched the wind blowing large chunks of ice across several areas of open water in the pond as I sipped my afternoon tea. Early spring was a bittersweet time for me. It was break-up season, which meant that ice fishing was over until next year. I'd taken down the fishing shanty at the first signs of thaw. No need to endanger myself or anyone else on thinning ice when we'd be out fishing on clear waters in a matter of weeks.

"The ice looks so pretty," my wife declared, handing me a cooled muffin from the sideboard. "The wind sweeps it into patterns and piles that melt together and then harden overnight."

"It's also dangerous," I pointed out before taking my first delicious bite. Mmm. Lemon with dried blueberries. Not as good as fresh ones, but I loved that my wife extended the season all winter by drying several batches of wild fruit for use all year. "Floating packs of ice can damage piers and pilings. We lost part of our dock to a mini-iceberg last year, remember?"

"I do. I helped you fix it," she said crisply. "I still think it's pretty!"

"I do too," I said placatingly. The missus was always right in our home.

THE SPECIAL

I finished my muffin and got ready for work. I had a position as a fireman on a freight train run for the Bangor and Aroostook Railroad and was currently working the evening shift. Our run took us from Jackman down to Greenville on an arm of the railroad owned by the Canadian Pacific. They ran a line from Montreal over to Saint John, New Brunswick, taking a shortcut through the United States since it was the fastest route from point A to point B. The Bangor and Aroostook Railroad had received permission to use a portion of this track for our freight, as long as every run was properly scheduled to avoid the CP trains. No one wanted any costly or life-threatening train accidents.

As soon as I arrived at the station, I got the engine's firebox loaded up with coal. By the time the freight cars were attached, the engine cab was nice and cozy. I settled in with the engineer to enjoy the ride, which we'd done half a hundred times or more this year. The snow was mostly gone, the tracks clear of ice, so there was nothing to worry about. We could relax and enjoy our routine run down to Greenville.

The engineer and I were discussing a large trout he had caught out on the ice as the steam train made its way up a long slope on the southeast side of Moosehead Lake. The engineer was interrupted mid-sentence by the wail of a train whistle piercing the chill night air. It must be a passing westbound train hailing us, as was the tradition on this remote line.

We both looked out of the window, startled by the noise. I'd checked the schedule before we left the station. There were no westbound trains scheduled at this hour. The engineer leaned out of the side window, gazing down the double tracks.

"It must be an unscheduled special," the engineer called to me. "But I can't see the train's headlight. It should be visible by now." He ducked his head back inside to navigate a gentle curve in the rail, then risked a quick glance back as the train straightened. He swore suddenly. "It's behind us."

I turned and gasped when I saw another train's headlight following us on the track. It was moving at high speed, the light shining ever brighter as the train drew near.

"It's going to rear-end us," I warned the engineer. "We need to increase our speed."

"Telegraph the switch operator," the engineer said, his voice tight. "I'm going to pull off at the next siding and let them go past."

I put the telegraph through, then started shoveling more coal into the firebox as the engineer poured on the speed. But the special was still outpacing us, the beams of its headlight pouring around either side of our freight cars.

"What *idiot* . . . scheduled a special . . . during a well-established freight run?" I panted as I shoveled.

"I don't know," the engineer roared back over the sound of the approaching locomotive. "But I will have words with that son-of-a-gun after this! If he doesn't slow down, he's going to run us off the tracks."

The engineer was keeping us just ahead of the special, but it was touch and go. The next available siding was just before the bridge over the river. If the operator hadn't reached the switchman, the special would rear-end us and both trains might skid off the tracks into the ravine.

The engineer braked for the switch, and the locomotive screeched and bucked as he turned us into the siding just before the bridge. We slid to a halt and watched in anger as the special roared past us on the main line. To my amazement, it only had two cars—the engine and the tender.

"What in tarnation?" the engineer shouted. "That drunken fool must be taking a joy ride!"

I just stared at the passing train, my mind frozen with astonishment. "What fool are you talking about?" I asked, my voice calmer than my nerves. "There's nobody in the engine."

The engineer's eyes widened. Then he swore and collapsed against the window, his face dripping with sweat.

At that moment, the switchman came running up, face pale and eyes wide. "Thank God you stopped," he shouted. "But how did you know to stop here? There wasn't any time to notify you. It just happened!"

I swung down out of the engine to meet him. "Notify us of what?" I asked.

"The bridge just collapsed," the switchman exclaimed. "A large ice floe jammed up against the supports and took out one of the main trestles."

I gasped and glanced up at the engineer, who was still leaning on the windowsill. His face turned ghost-white and his whole body started trembling. I turned back to the switchman. "We didn't know about the bridge," I replied. "We pulled onto the switch to get away from the special that was harassing us. We thought it was going to run us off the tracks."

The switchman frowned. "What special?" he asked.

"The one that passed just now," I said testily. There was no way the man could have missed seeing the second locomotive. He'd been staring directly at our train, and the special had passed right next to us.

The switchman gave me a strange look and then carefully looked up and down the empty track. "I didn't see another train," he said cautiously. "There's no one else scheduled on the rails tonight."

The engineer climbed down to meet us. "There's only one way to find out," he said to me, ignoring the hovering switchman. "Either that durned special just crashed into the river or . . ."

He didn't finish his sentence, and I wasn't sure I wanted him to.

"We would have heard it crash," I protested. I waved to the rest of our crew, signaling for them to stay with the freight train, then I followed the engineer, who stomped along the tracks toward the river. The switchman jogged behind us. He still seemed baffled by this turn of events. That made two of us.

In a few moments, the broken remains of the bridge came into view. It had completely collapsed, and its tangled remains were caught up among the great floes of ice that lined both sides of the river. There was no sign of the special train that had tailed us down from Jackman. It had vanished like . . . well, like a ghost.

I sat down abruptly on the side of the tracks as the reality of the situation finally penetrated my agitated brain. "Dear God," I gasped. "We would be at the bottom of that river right now if we hadn't stopped on the siding."

"That's what I said," grumbled the switchman.

The engineer sat down beside me, and we stared in horror at the broken bridge.

"Would someone explain to me what just happened?" the switchman begged.

We told him. When we reached the part where the special train roared past the siding, heading straight for the broken bridge, he sat down too. I think his legs gave out.

"So, was it a phantom train?" he asked. "Is that why I couldn't see it?"

"I don't know what else it could be," I said honestly.

"That phantom train just saved the lives of everyone aboard our locomotive," the engineer said crisply. "I'd call that a miracle." He stood up, brushed off his pants, and headed back toward the train.

I couldn't top that statement and didn't try. I helped the astonished switchman to his feet and followed. I still felt a bit shaky, but mostly I was grateful. I had a whole lot more living to do, and now I could do it, thanks to the phantom train.

4

The Girl in the Graveyard

BRUNSWICK

My buddy Tyler and I were driving back to Bowdoin one evening after our weekly poker game at his cousin's place. I was feeling mighty pleased with life. I'd won the final hand and had a nice stack of bills in my jacket pocket to prove it.

Tyler was a bit out of sorts, because some of those bills had once been his. And they might still be again next week, I pointed out a bit smugly.

"Dan, pull over," Tyler said suddenly. I jammed on the brakes, looking around wildly for the emergency. But the streets were dark and silent, the only thing of note was the cemetery sprawling to one side of us. And then I saw what he meant. There was a pretty girl in old-fashioned clothes standing forlornly just inside the cemetery fence. She was about our age, and she looked as if she had been attending an upscale costume party until her date abandoned her for another girl.

As if he'd read my thoughts, Tyler said: "Poor girl. Her boyfriend left her in the lurch. Let's give her a ride. Save her paying for a taxi."

THE GIRL IN THE GRAVEYARD

I glanced at Tyler. His eyes had a sparkle that told me he found this girl attractive. He'd just gone through a breakup and was looking for someone new. He may have found her.

Tyler jumped out of the passenger door and called out: "Miss, do you need a ride?"

The girl smiled with relief and stepped away from the cemetery fence. "I do, yes."

Tyler introduced himself and then me. I waved at her from the driver's seat. The girl said her name was Jane Brown.

As Tyler held the back door open, I noticed that the girl was shivering. "Here miss, take my jacket," I said, shrugging it off and handing it over the seat. She thanked me with a dazzling smile that made me a little dizzy.

If Tyler didn't ask for her number, I would.

My buddy swung into the passenger seat and buckled up. As I put on the blinker and edged back onto the road, he asked the girl for her address.

"Please drop me off at McKeen Street," she said softly. "I need to go home."

She must commute to college, I thought, pausing at a red light. Probably trying to save money.

Glancing at her in the rearview mirror, I thought the fancy costume looked a bit large on her frail frame. She was far too pale, almost skeletal in appearance. Someone needed to get a few good meals into her. As if she sensed my gaze, the girl shivered and pulled my jacket tighter around her shoulders.

Tyler leaned over the seat, smiling admiringly at the girl and trying to engage her in conversation, but her monosyllabic answers told us both she wasn't interested in talking.

Disappointed, my buddy turned away and put on some music to pass the short drive to McKeen Street.

When we reached her road, the girl directed me toward one of the houses. "Please don't pull into the driveway," she said. "My parents are light sleepers, and I don't want them to know I was out so late." I stopped in front of her house, and she thanked us both and exited the car. Tyler got out too and saw her to the door, but the slump in his shoulders told me he had no luck getting her number. Too bad. She had a beautiful smile.

I turned the conversation to poker as we drove back to Bowdoin. It wasn't until I reached my dorm room and reached for my winnings that I realized they were still in the pocket of my jacket. And my jacket was in a small house on McKeen Street. The girl in the costume had forgotten to return it. Oh well. We could go back tomorrow and get it, I thought.

I had two classes the next morning, so it was lunchtime when Tyler and I drove back to McKeen Street. There was a car in the driveway, so someone should be home. I could tell from my buddy's face that he was hoping it was the girl. But a tall man with thinning hair, worried wrinkles, and stooped shoulders answered instead.

"Good afternoon, Mr. Brown," I said in my politest tones. "Tyler and I gave your daughter a ride home last night, and she forgot to return my sports jacket when she went inside. I was hoping I could get it back."

The man frowned at me, clearly puzzled by this request. "Son, I don't have a daughter. Not anymore. You say you dropped a girl off at this property last night?"

Glancing over his shoulder, I saw a fancy painting on the wall facing the door. "Not just any girl," I replied. "That girl right there. Isn't Jane your daughter?" I pointed to the picture.

The man glanced at the portrait and the color drained out of his face. His knees buckled, and Tyler and I each grabbed an arm and helped him to a bench beside an old-fashioned umbrella stand. "Sir, are you all right?" I exclaimed. "Can I get you a drink of water?"

"No, no. I'm fine, son. It was just a bit of a shock," Mr. Brown said. "The girl in that portrait *is* my daughter Jane, but she died in a car accident thirty years ago."

I gasped and my knees started to wobble. I landed on the bench beside the man.

"I'm sorry to hear that," Tyler said, his face as pale as a ghost. "We are so sorry to trouble you, sir. Come on, Dan. Let's go."

I rose shakily. "We apologize for taking up your time," I said to the man, who looked as if he was about to cry.

We drove away as fast as possible. Once we were off McKeen Street, I found the closest coffee shop and pulled into the lot. I was hyperventilating with shock and fear.

"What just happened?!" I exclaimed so loudly Tyler slapped his hands over his ears. I repeated the question in a more reasonable tone, and Tyler replied: "As far as I can figure it, either that girl was messing around or . . ."

Shivers ran up and down my spine. "Or?" I asked in a sharp tone.

"Or we just gave a ride to a ghost," Tyler said.

At his words, my whole body started shaking. Sometimes I really hated my buddy's practical approach to life. Even the supernatural didn't shake him.

Tyler grabbed a bottle of water from the case in the back seat and made me drink the whole thing. "Get in the passenger seat," he commanded. "You are in no fit state to drive."

He was right about that. As he walked around the car, I crawled awkwardly into the next seat and opened a second bottle of water.

Unfortunately for my nerves, the closest route to my next class led past one side of the cemetery where we'd met Jane Brown. I glanced nervously toward the graveyard and saw a flash of color on one of the gravestones. It was . . . no, it couldn't be. Yes, it could.

"Tyler, pull over," I shouted.

Tyler jammed on the brakes, looking around wildly for the emergency. I leapt out of the car and ran through the trees and vaulted the fence. I jogged three rows back and four over, landing next to a gravestone near the center. My sports jacket was draped carefully across the top of the stone, and my poker winnings were still in the pocket. As Tyler came panting up to me, I stared at the words engraved on the stone. It said: "R.I.P. Jane Brown."

5

Weird Helmsman

SCHOONER HEAD

ACADIA NATIONAL PARK

The captain watched as the last boxes of spices, gold, and other goods captured in the Bahamas were loaded onto the small schooner. His orders were clear: sail up to Mount Desert Island and add this shipment to the treasure cache their leader, the famed pirate Captain Kidd, had stored there. Don't get caught.

It was an easy, safe journey at that time of year, so the captain brought his wife along. There was some unease among the rough pirate crew at having a woman aboard, which was considered bad luck. But the skipper did not hold with such nonsense. He had sailed more than once with a crew numbering thirteen, and no harm had come to anyone on his pirate ship, although the same could not be said of the merchant vessels they encountered. So, the captain ignored the grumbling and gave the order to set sail.

The winds were swift and the sea kind on the journey northward. It was only when they came abreast of the coast of Maine that a dense fog set in. It was so heavy that the sailor on the forecastle could scarcely see to the end of the jib. The breeze was light and steady, pushing the small schooner deeper into the fog.

WEIRD HELMSMAN

The pirate captain stood by the wheel, keeping watch with his men. Fog at sea was never a friend, and this was particularly true when a ship was filled with ill-gotten treasure, and its crew were buccaneers wanted in every port along the eastern coast. He motioned the crew to silence, for they would not see any passing ship in this mist. A loud shout, a whistle, or even the toll of the watch bell could give away their presence and endanger their mission.

It was dusk when a brisk wind dissipated the fog. The lookout gave a sudden shout, and all eyes turned windward. The captain swore as he beheld a British corvette a few miles away.

They had been spotted by the corvette, which fired a signal asking them to heave to for boarding. The captain swore again. All the ships they'd encountered previously had assumed they were a merchant bound for Maine. It was just their bad luck to encounter a suspicious captain who wanted to verify their "good intentions."

The pirate captain ordered his crew to outrun the corvette. They adjusted the sails to take best advantage of the new breeze, and accelerated away from the British ship. The small schooner was much lighter than their heavy pursuer, and the distance between the two vessels lengthened.

The captain's wife came on deck when she felt the change in speed, her eyes wide with fear. His rough features softened at the sight of her lovely face, and he whispered reassurances before firmly escorting her back to his cabin, out of sight of the superstitious crew.

"What can I do?" she whispered.

"Pray," the captain said. He was not a believing man, but his wife needed something to hang on to. She nodded, and he left her on her knees beside the bunk.

The wind grew fierce as darkness fell. The sea tossed the light schooner like a bath toy, giving the heavier corvette an advantage. As the gap closed between the vessels, the British began firing upon the pirate schooner. Not good.

The captain ordered the helmsman to steer closer to land, where they had a better chance of eluding their pursuers among the inlets and coves where hidden ledges and shoals might harm the larger vessel. Behind them, the random shots from the British corvette landed in the waters around the schooner, each a little closer than the last.

"Make for the cove," the captain shouted. The crew knew where he meant. Locals called it Otter Cove. It was the closest landing to their hidden trove. The pirate captain hoped to ferry their treasure ashore in the boats and scuttle the ship while the British searched for them among the islets of Frenchman's Bay. The crew could escape overland to Southwest Harbor, where one of Kidd's retainers kept watch. They would commandeer another ship on which the crew could escape.

This plan was swiftly foiled when a gale-force wind roared down upon the small schooner. The crew worked fiercely as huge waves rose and fell around them, sails straining to keep pace. Tide, waves, and wind conspired against the pirate ship, and they swept past the sought-after cove.

The pirate captain scanned the night-darkened coastline with his glass, seeking another cove or inlet where they could hide. To his left, a shot from the pursuing British corvette splashed just off the stern. The heavier ship had the advantage on this boisterous eve.

Then the pirate captain spotted a whitish glimmer ahead in the dark. It was the looked-for gap in the rocky coastline!

He shouted the heading above the roaring wind, and the crew turned the ship, speeding landward at eight knots. The small schooner leapt nimbly for the gap in the shore and its promised safety, the crew inspired to new heights by hope.

Then the crashing sound of breakers reached their ears, warning captain and crew that the supposed "inlet" was only a trick of the light. They were sailing directly toward a cliff face made up of rocks of a whitish tint.

"Turn the ship!" the captain screamed in horror. But at that moment, a random shot from the British corvette knocked over the helmsman and passed through the main halyards. The mainsail plummeted to the deck, hampering the desperate crew.

The captain threw himself behind the wheel and turned the ship as fast as his hands would move. But it was too late. With the sail down, the crew in disarray, and ledges on all sides, the pirate ship was doomed. Grim-faced pirates worked the ropes and sails, trying to save themselves from this dread fate.

The captain strained his eyes against the darkness, searching for a beach of any kind across the seething waters. The tide was going out, so there might yet be a stretch of land where he could scuttle the ship. If he could get the schooner close enough to shore, his wife at least might survive this night.

As if summoned by the thought, she appeared at his side, hairpins gone, face resigned. Her dark hair streamed around them as the pirate captain aimed the bow of the ship between two rugged ledges, glimpsing a weedy curve of mud beyond. But a large wave rose behind them, lifting the fragile schooner as if it weighed no more than a feather and thumping it cruelly onto the ledge beneath the Spouting Head.

The foremast cracked and fell overboard, and two pirates manning the forecastle leapt onto it and scrambled desperately along it to the rocks at the edge of the cliff. Before anyone else could follow, another wave washed the splintered mast backward into the pitiless sea.

The captain's wife knelt beside the wheel, her pale face twisted with despair, and prayed aloud for the souls of those aboard the doomed ship. Relentless waves pushed and pulled the ship to pieces, slamming it repeatedly on the rocks. Finally, a rogue wave appeared like a foam-crested monster above the wreckage of the schooner and dragged the shattered remains backward into the sea, killing all aboard.

The lookout on the British corvette, who was watching the ship from a safe distance, gasped in shock when the vessel vanished suddenly from view. "The schooner disappeared," he told his captain, eyes wide with dread. "I fear we have been chasing a ghost."

"Nonsense," the captain said crisply. "The gale has impaired your vision." Nevertheless, he gave orders for the corvette to retreat to a sheltered location for the remainder of the night.

At dawn, the British ship returned to the headland, but there were no signs of the ill-fated pirate schooner. It had vanished without a trace.

On moonlit nights when the fog rises across land and sea, locals occasionally see a phantom ship at Schooner Head. The vessel sails out of the mist, speeding toward the headland where once it sank, sails straining against unseen gale-force winds. A weird helmsman kneels before the wheel, her dark hair streaming in the phantom breeze, her face twisted with grief. When the ship reaches the ledge below the Spouting Head, it disappears.

6

Hope Chest

BANGOR

"What are you looking at, Grandma?" I asked from the doorway of the spare bedroom. My grandmother sat on the rag rug in front of an old seaman's chest with its lid open. The trunk had sat nearly forever under the window overlooking the backyard, and I'd never once seen it open. Grandma held a yellowing piece of paper in her hand. She smiled and turned the page to show me a sketch of a girl who looked somewhat like myself.

"Is that you?" I asked, plunking down beside her.

"It is. You got your name *and* your good looks from me," she joked, patting her graying blond hair. I laughed. She handed me the sketch and started rifling through the old trunk. Old-fashioned clothing. A small jewelry box with a few necklaces and rings.

"Who drew this sketch?" I asked.

"A man named Joe," Grandma said, suddenly solemn. "And therein lies a tale." She reached deep into the trunk and pulled out a sketchbook and a box full of pencils. She handed me the book. I paged through sketch after sketch of pine woods, the Penobscot River, and multiple angles of an old farmhouse. I

HOPE CHEST

even found the place where the picture of my grandma had been carefully removed.

"We were going to get that picture framed and hang it on the wall of our new house when we married," she said.

"You and Granddad? Why didn't you?"

"Not me and Granddad. Me and Joe," Grandma said.

"You and *Joe*? You were going to marry Joe who drew this sketch?"

"I was supposed to. Come on. We may as well get comfy," Grandma said. "This is a long story."

She collected the sketchbook from me and went to sit on the quilt-covered bed. I sat beside her with the drawing in my hand.

Gesturing toward the open trunk, Grandma said, "Those are the clothes I wore as a young girl living in Bangor, Maine."

"I lived in a town on the Penobscot River, and I loved it. Never thought I would leave." As she continued speaking, I could picture the long-ago scene in my mind.

Young Ella was a beauty and her papa had some money. All the local lads had their eye on Ella, and she never lacked for a partner at village dances. But none of the local fellows suited her. Things changed when Joe came to town. He'd lost his health at a city job, and his doctor sent him to the country to heal. Joe boarded with a farmer just down the road from Ella's home and took work trading horses and dickering for folks who didn't have the knack. He was a well-spoken fellow and folks liked him.

Joe attended the local church and the local dances, and soon he was courting Ella along with half the boys in town. Ella took a real shine to Joe. When he came to the farm one day to ask for her hand in marriage, she accepted right away.

"Pa and Ma really liked Joe," Grandma said. She showed me the sketch of a happy older couple on the penultimate page. "And this is Joe." The last page showed a flashy young man with a dashing air. The picture made me uneasy. The man's eyes looked a bit narrow and shifty. A frisson of fear raised goose bumps along my arms as Grandma continued her tale.

Joe called at the old farmhouse almost every evening to visit with Ella and plan their wedding. It was around that time that strange things started happening on the farm. A sturdy shelf fell off the wall and nearly hit Joe on the head. The porch swing broke as soon as he sat on it. The autumn wind would bang the shutters so loud you couldn't hear Joe speak.

When the weather turned cold, the affianced couple spent each evening in the parlor with Ella's folks as chaperones. That's when it became apparent that they had a ghost. When everyone sat down with the tea tray, loud banging noises started up in the attic. The men went upstairs to investigate, but nothing was there. Some evenings, the fire in the hearth would blow out suddenly, as if doused with a bucket of water. The room temperature dropped so dramatically that Joe was forced to cut his visit short. One night, a grinding sound came from the roof. It sounded like someone had climbed up and started shoveling off the shingles. Everyone trooped outside to look, but there was nothing there.

Ella and her family were terrified of the noisy specter, and the haunting became the talk of the town. No family member was hurt by the phantom. The same could not be said for Joe. The teapot launched itself at his head one evening, spilling tea all over the parlor. Chairs broke almost every time he sat on them. One frigid evening, when Joe and Ella came in from a snowy walk and stood warming themselves by the kitchen stove, a rat-a-tat-tat sound like a drumbeat descended from the ceiling and surrounded them. Ella's mama dropped the paring knife into the pie plate and clapped her hands to her ears. The sound grew louder and the temperature in the kitchen plummeted. The stove fire went out with a bang.

"I'm sorry, Ella, I've got to go. Forgot an appointment in town," Joe gabbled, kissing her hastily and rushing out the back door. As soon as he left the property, the sound stopped.

Ella's father came into the kitchen. He put his arm around his trembling wife and looked grimly at his daughter. "My child, you do realize that strange things keep happening every time that young man comes to the farm?" he asked.

Ella pulled out her handkerchief, blew her nose, and nodded.

"You were named for my mother, who passed before you were born. I think it is your grandmother's ghost who is trying to tell us something," her father said. "Many of the noises have their origins in the attic. I was up there just now and found the old seaman's trunk that my mother used as her hope chest. That drumming sound we heard started inside the old trunk the moment Joe stepped into the yard and it traveled downstairs when he crossed the threshold. I was following the sound to see what would happen."

Ella wanted to protest, but she couldn't deny that something was very wrong. She reluctantly agreed to break things off with Joe.

Ella's father summoned the young man the next morning, and—over rattling bangs from the attic—told Joe the engagement was ended and he was no longer welcome at the farm. Joe protested mightily, begging to see Ella, and asking for a second chance—until the portrait of Ella's grandmother ripped itself off the wall and launched itself at him. Then Joe shrieked and ran from the room. The portrait landed with a thud on the porch, and the eyes watched Joe until he vanished around the curve in the road.

With the departure of Ella's betrothed, the farmhouse became a peaceful haven. No banging noises, no falling shelves, no breaking furniture. Grandmother's portrait stayed firmly on the wall.

Ella pined for her lost love, losing weight and color. She stopped going to the local dances, not wishing to watch the other girls flirting with Joe, now that he was a free man. The whole town couldn't stop talking about the ghost who threw out Ella's fiancé. The story cast Joe into the role of a hero because he'd survived the haunting. The local girls were cold toward Ella and her family when they came to church on Sunday, but the older couples just laughed and speculated on what it meant. And the young fellows were glad that they had another chance with the prettiest girl in town.

About a month after the breakup, a stranger arrived on the stagecoach and started asking questions around the neighborhood. In a matter of hours, Joe was arrested and taken away. He'd abandoned a young wife, stolen a large amount of money, and was hiding from the law. And there were other charges against him that Ella's father refused to discuss.

Ella was devastated all over again. How could she have been fooled by such a rogue? She almost married a bigamist and a thief. She was so distraught that her father sent her to stay with his sister, who had married a banker from Dayton, until Ella recovered her strength and her spirits.

"At Pa's request, Mama packed all my belongings into my grandmother's hope chest," Grandma said. "Pa said he'd feel better about sending me away if I had my grandmother's ghost along to keep an eye on me."

"That's her, isn't it?" I said, gesturing toward the portrait of an eighteenth-century lady on the wall. "Is that the picture that chased Joe out of the house?"

Grandma laughed. "Yes, it is," she said.

"I met your granddad during my trip," she continued. "I guess your grandma decided he was the right man for me, because her ghost locked us both in my aunt's woodshed and wouldn't let us out until your grandfather proposed!"

"And I will always be grateful to the lady ghost for that," Granddad said from the doorway. He came into the room and gave Grandma a long kiss. I looked away, embarrassed, and I swear that the portrait of my great-great-grandmother winked at me.

The window banged open suddenly. A breeze whipped into the room and snatched Joe's sketch of my grandmother off the bed. "Hey, give that back!" I shouted. I tried to grab it, but it swirled out of reach and sailed out the window. Before my astonished eyes, the sketch ripped itself into tiny pieces and the wind chased those pieces out of the yard. The sketchbook rose and placed itself back into the trunk. The lid closed with a determined bang.

"Ella, meet your great-great-grandmother," Granddad said with a laugh. "She *still* doesn't like Joe!"

I sank down on the bed, my legs trembling. I wasn't sure I approved of ghosts. Even if they were family.

"When you get serious about someone, make sure you bring the fellow over here to meet your grandma and me," Granddad added. "And let the first Ella get a good look at him. She'll know if everything's all right."

As Grandma swept us downstairs for cookies and hot tea, I thought about Granddad's offer. Actually, I might take him up on that. I didn't want to fall for someone like Joe. Better to be safe than sorry.

7

Do You Need a Shave?

EASTPORT

The tin peddler drove his wagon down the twilight road, brushing irritably at overhanging branches that occasionally deposited wet droplets down his neck. Fog was rolling in from the sea, and he was eager to get out of the elements. His final customer of the day, a local farmer, had purchased a costly new stove pipe and recommended lodging for the night at a nearby tavern. So, he had set off through the mist and the mud in search of food and shelter. When his weary horse reached the top of a low hill, the peddler saw a light glowing through the mist. Here was the much-anticipated tavern, at last.

The peddler took his horse and wagon directly to the stable yard. He locked up his goods and paid the ostler to take care of his horse. Then he walked through the yard in the mist and raindrops, listening to the babble of voices coming from the comfortable building.

When the peddler stepped inside the warm barroom, he was hailed immediately by the landlord. The peddler requested a meal and a room for the night. One of these—the meal—the landlord was happy to supply, but he had no room left to rent.

DO YOU NEED A SHAVE?

"No room anywhere?" asked the peddler. "I don't think my horse can go any further. Surely there is a spare place for a single person to sleep? A spare room? A couch in a corner? I can pay well."

A look of dismay crossed the landlord's face, then quickly banished. But the peddler had seen it and pressed harder. At last, the landlord said he could stay the night, if he was willing to sleep in an unused spare room that was rumored to be haunted. The landlord looked a bit sheepish when he said it, but he stuck to his story when the peddler stared at him in disbelief.

"Haunted how? Who or what is doing the haunting?" asked the peddler, when he realized the landlord was serious.

"Haunted by the ghost of a barber," said the landlord. "He was murdered in that very room a decade ago, long before I purchased the business. Ever since that fateful day, anyone who retires in that room hears a voice wailing: "Do you need a shave?" The landlord shivered as he spoke.

The peddler repressed a smile. He said: "Very well. I am loath to travel further this evening, so I will rent the barber's room. I am not afraid of ghosts. If he comes to me tonight, I will let him shave me."

After paying the landlord a goodly sum, the peddler sat down in the tavern to a hearty meal of stew and hot bread. When he finished, he asked the landlord to show him to the barber's room. The landlord led him up the stairs and through a large room where several seamen were seated at a gambling table, laughing and swearing at one another. The peddler skirted the merry group and walked down a narrow hallway at the landlord's heels. He entered a small room with a bed, a chest of drawers, a large table with a pitcher and a bowl, and a smaller bedside table with an oil lamp. The landlord lit the lamp and took the pitcher downstairs with him to fetch some warm water so the peddler could wash.

The peddler unpacked his saddlebag, accepted the pitcher of water from the landlord, and then spent five minutes looking into every nook and crevice in the room to assure himself that he was alone and no murdered barber shared the space with him. Laughing at himself, the peddler washed up, donned his nightshirt, and lay down on the bed.

The peddler was almost asleep when a voice echoed through the small chamber. "Do . . . you . . . need . . . a . . . shave?" He sat bolt upright in bed, heart thumping wildly, all sleepiness gone in an instant. Jumping out of bed, he turned on the lamp and searched every corner of the room. He found nothing. Taking a few deep breaths, the peddler went back to bed.

Several minutes passed without incident. The peddler decided it was a dream spawned by the landlord's ghostly tale. He turned over, preparing himself to sleep.

"Do . . . you . . . need . . . a . . . shave?" a voice moaned.

The shocked peddler leapt straight out of the bed. He patted his way around the dark room, feeling into every corner and even crawling under the bed. No one was there. Finally, he stood at the center of the room, holding the pitcher of water before him like a weapon, waiting for the voice.

"Do . . . you . . . need . . . a . . . shave?" the voice creaked and groaned. Now that he was fully awake, the peddler realized there was something strange about the voice. It seemed louder near the window. He put down the pitcher, walked to the window, and opened it.

"Do . . . you . . . need . . . a . . . shave?" the voice said in his ear. The peddler gasped and threw himself back toward the bed. He stood shaking from head to toe, but he was determined to solve this mystery. If it was a ghost, he would repeat scripture verses until it left. But he suspected there was a more natural explanation for the sound.

The peddler went back to the window and peered out into the fog. There was a large oak tree beside the house, and one limb was just below the window. As he peered down at it, a gust of wind shook the tree, and the limb scraped the side of the tavern. The tree groaned as it bent and shivered, and the peddler decided this must be the source of the "barber's ghost." If someone sleeping in the haunted room heard the tree groaning, they would assume it was the barber's spirit and investigate no further.

Satisfied, the peddler went back to bed, ignoring the spectral voice whenever it wailed its ghostly question: "Do . . . you . . . need . . . a . . . shave?"

The tin peddler was almost asleep when a shout of laughter came from the gamblers in the room down the hall. Someone had won a good hand. He frowned and rolled over, but the noise level continued to rise, preventing sleep. The sailors argued and swore and laughed and yelled as the ale flowed and the game grew ever more rowdy. The peddler was annoyed. If this continued, he would get no sleep tonight. Then, he was struck by an idea. Maybe he could use the story of the barber's ghost to his advantage! The gamblers would surely have heard the tale from the landlord and believed it too, not knowing about the groaning tree branch just outside the window.

The tin peddler stripped the sheet off the bed, draped a towel over his shoulder in the typical barber fashion, emptied the washbasin out the window, and then carefully cradled it in his arms in his best barber imitation. He crept down the narrow hallway and stood outside the door to the gambler's room, waiting for a lull in the game. When things quieted for a moment, he kicked open the door, which hit the wall with a loud bang. Stalking boldly into the room, he intoned: "Do . . . you . . . need . . . a . . . shave?"

There was a moment of stunned silence. The gamblers stared in shock at the ghostly figure in the doorway. Then they screamed in unison and bolted for the door at the far end of the room, tumbling over themselves in their mad dash to escape down the stairs. They kicked up such a breeze that the sheet nearly blew off the peddler's head.

In a matter of seconds, the peddler was alone in the room. At the center of the table was the stake from the disrupted game. The peddler estimated that it was close to a thousand dollars. He calmly scooped it up in his washbowl and returned to his room.

A gold coin dropped to the floor as he placed the cash into his money belt, and he spent several minutes trying to reach it underneath the heavy chest of drawers before he finally gave up. It was a small loss compared to what he had gained from his prank. The peddler lay down, pulled the blanket over his head, and went to sleep, happily ignoring the ghostly groans overhead.

When he went to breakfast the next morning, the peddler found the tavern filled with wide-eyed customers gossiping about the ghost that had disrupted the gamblers during the night. The landlord asked the peddler if he had seen the ghost.

"The spirit did not trouble me," the peddler said.

"You were lucky," the landlord said, setting breakfast in front of him. "It manifested in front of the gamblers last night and several people were injured trying to escape."

The peddler ate quickly, paid what remained of his bill, and went out into the stable yard to retrieve his rig. The fog was lifting as he passed below the window of his rented room. Into the morning quiet, a voice overhead inquired: "Do . . . you . . . need . . . a . . . shave?" The peddler stopped in his tracks and looked up at the tree. No breeze was stirring. The branch above him was completely still.

A voice spoke directly into his ear: "Do . . . you . . . need . . . a . . . shave?"

The peddler whirled and stared into the translucent face of the phantom barber, who was hovering beside him.

"I do not need a shave," he screamed, scrambling away from the barber's floating form. "In the name of God, go away!"

The peddler charged toward the stables, not pausing to see what effect his words had upon the phantom. He thrust a huge tip upon the ostler, who got his rig ready in record time.

The peddler drove out of the stable yard at a brisk trot, never looking back at the haunted tavern. Which was a pity. If he had risked a glance, the peddler would have seen the barber's ghost hovering in the upstairs window, curiously examining the gold coin that had fallen beneath the chest of drawers.

8

The Photograph

LONG LAKE

When J. P. suggested a trip to Maine over a poker game one evening, our whole group was excited. We all loved to fish, and J. P.'s cousin had a place on Long Lake that was big enough to room ten. So, five couples made the journey north in early July, our cars full of bags, books, and fishing poles. While we planned to fish, our wives were eager to read, boat, and shop. Not necessarily in that order.

The cabin was almost palatial, something J. P. neglected to mention. My wife made everyone take off their shoes before entering the place. We all gawked at the view of the water, which had a big dock. Bags were rather haphazardly dumped into various rooms so folks could get into their swimming gear and get the party started.

Al was the last one down, as always. He was an amateur photographer, and he'd been snapping photos from the minute we crossed the state line.

"Put the camera in that chair by the tree," J. P. yelled from the water. "You don't want to ruin it."

"Ruin it how? I'm nowhere near the water," Al protested as he carefully laid his equipment in the prescribed place.

THE PHOTOGRAPH

As soon as Al's fancy camera was safe, two of our poker buddies jumped him from behind and tossed him into the lake. Al came up sputtering in indignation, and everyone laughed. We swam and played water games and drank beer as if we were crazy college students on holiday instead of respectable businessmen. It was fun.

The next few days were spent fishing, lounging, and grilling. We'd rented several boats, and one or another of the wives often joined our fishing parties. One day, I borrowed a car and took my wife to the shore, where we ate lunch at a romantic restaurant and visited several lighthouses.

When we returned from our excursion, the whole group was abuzz.

"What's going on?" I asked as I carried several bags of souvenirs into the house.

"One of the neighbors just told J. P. about a haunted farmhouse not far from here," Al exclaimed. "They have arranged for us to see the place if the weather holds."

"Ghosts, huh?" I asked, exchanging glances with my wife. She was not keen on anything spooky.

"We are going during the day," J. P. called from a lounge chair. "The locals won't go near the place at night."

My wife relaxed and nodded. "Sounds good," I said easily.

When I returned from stowing our new possessions, I grabbed a beer from the refrigerator and asked about the haunted house.

"It's a dilapidated old farmhouse that hasn't been used in decades," J. P. said. "According to local rumors, the last owner was a bad lot, very cruel to his wife. Beat her, starved her, kicked her out a few times. She kept coming back, said she wanted to die in that house so she could haunt it—and the old man—forever afterward. She said she was going to stick it to him good and proper in the afterlife, and that's just what happened. Locals say you can hear moaning and weeping and maniacal laughter coming from the place. Sometimes a misty figure appears in the window."

"Sounds like the perfect vacation spot," my wife said dryly. "When do we go?"

"Tomorrow morning," J. P. said. "Wear hiking clothes. We are going up a mountain."

"What joy," Al's wife said. She clinked beer glasses with my wife, and they chuckled together. I was very glad we'd married such adventurous ladies. Otherwise, they'd never have put up with our nonsense.

All ten of us loaded into the cars the next morning and drove to the meeting place. The neighbor had arranged for his sister to show us the way to the haunted house. The young woman led us up a steep mountain path that opened into an overgrown field. A rotting farmhouse partially set back into some pine trees came into view. The young woman briskly directed us toward the building but refused to accompany us any further. She said she'd seen the spirit once herself and had no desire to become reacquainted with it.

By the time we'd chivied Al and his bulky camera over a teetering fence, the young woman was speeding down the hill, almost at a run. That did not bode well. My wife grabbed my arm and held on tight as we climbed toward the ruined building. I was pretty sure it wasn't the weeds or the uneven footing that disturbed her. "I don't like this place," she whispered in my ear. "It feels off."

It certainly was eerie. Splintered fencing surrounded the weedy yard, and the somber house had a sagging roof, collapsed side porch, and large dark holes gaping randomly in the walls. The farmhouse should have been condemned, but no one in the region wanted anything to do with the haunted property, so it just rotted away, decade after decade.

The sun went behind a cloud as our ghost-viewing party edged through a creaky gate that squealed when Al opened it. A cool breeze swept through the hovering pine trees, which swayed and groaned. Dead pine needles showered down upon us, and everyone shivered. No wonder there were ghost stories about this place. The whispering pines, the decaying house, and the tangled shrubbery in the overgrown yard created an atmosphere that was ripe for scary stories, even in the daylight.

J. P. was already at the front door, trying to figure out how to get everyone safely into the house since the steps were long gone. He gave me a boost through the door, and I caught folks as he swung them up to me. Between the two of us, we managed to maneuver everyone into the front room of the haunted house. It was a grimy, worn-out sitting room full of rotten furnishings and animal droppings. Cobwebs hung in every corner, and the dust on the windowpanes dimmed what little light was filtering through the massing storm clouds.

"Spooky," Al said enthusiastically. He raised his camera, took a couple of steps forward, and fell through the groaning floorboards. His wife gave a cry of dismay, and we hastily pulled him up, wiping away rotting splinters that littered his clothes.

"Are you hurt?" his wife asked.

"Not at all," he assured her, somewhat shakily. His main concern was his fancy camera. He checked it thoroughly while the rest of us tested the floorboards to make sure they would hold.

Our group walked slowly through the downstairs rooms. The kitchen had a broken iron stove and a pump in the sink. It was filled with pine needles and dead bugs, which made more than one person squeal. Through the cracks in a small window, I saw the remains of an outhouse. A rickety table trembled with every footstep, the splintered remains of a bench creaking beneath it.

"Do not touch that," I warned Al, who had enthusiastically approached a blackened fireplace in search of an interesting angle. "Those bricks are loose." He nodded distractedly and I sighed. Al never listened to safety tips. Photography would kill him one day.

"The phantom is usually seen in an upper window," J. P. said, looking up the dusty stairwell. "Let's go up!"

"Let's not," muttered my wife, but J. P. was already creeping slowly upward, testing out each step.

"All clear," he called from the top.

One by one, each couple in our group followed. I stayed at the rear with my trembling wife. "If anything happens, make a run for it. The door in the kitchen has only one step down. Go that way," I whispered.

"Just a couple of bedrooms," J. P. reported from somewhere ahead. "Not much to see really. Broken down beds, and it looks like a rat made a nest in this closet." He was speaking in a jovial fashion, but there was an underlying note of strain. This upper story felt very wrong.

I glanced into the bedroom facing the rear. Glass from the shattered window was all over the floor, so I motioned for my wife to stay in the hallway. The bedroom facing the front yard was the ghostly hotspot, so our group crowded inside in hopes of a sighting. We surrounded the ancient bed and Al leaned against a worn wardrobe, eyes fixed on the spectral window, heavy camera hanging from the strap around his neck. J. P. knelt on the floor beside a seaman's chest under the window, trying to open it.

"Nothing's happening, J. P.," his wife said. She sneezed delicately and pressed a handkerchief to her dripping nose. The room was dusty and cold. Far too cold for autumn.

"This chest is locked," J. P. said distractedly. "I should have brought some tools."

I blinked in surprise when I saw puffs of vapor emerge from his mouth with each word. The coldness deepened around us, and several folks shivered. "I don't like it in here," Al's wife whispered. "Let's go downstairs."

That's when the noises began. From a dark corner came the snap of a whip. It sounded like someone was thrashing the seaman's chest. J. P. scrambled backward like a crab and crashed into me. I pulled him to his feet, as everyone gasped in horror. A spectral voice moaned in pain as the whip cracked again and again. A scream of terror was followed by a menacing chuckle that rapidly increased in volume until we were clutching our ears. My knees trembled with fear, and my stomach roiled in panic.

My wife squeezed my shoulder once, our private signal, and I heard her hurrying away to safety. At that moment, the sounds ceased abruptly. I took a deep breath, then held it when a mist formed in the corner, twisting itself into the figure of a woman hovering above the sea chest. I could see her quite clearly, though I could also see the window frame right through her body. A ray of sun peeked out through the storm clouds and its beams pierced through the ghost's ectoplasm. I took one look at her vengeful smile and fled after my wife.

The others followed me pell-mell down the stairs. Behind us, I could hear the whip striking its victim once again. Moans and menacing laughter filled the house as I ran through the kitchen and out the back door. When I entered the yard, the sounds ceased.

I raced around to the front of the house and saw my wife running through the field. She had almost reached the mountain path we'd climbed earlier this morning. Behind me, I heard a frustrated yell. "Al," screamed his wife. "This is no time to take pictures."

I whirled around as J. P. and his wife slid past me, aiming for the mountain path. There was Al, standing at the gate, lining up a picture of the haunted farmhouse with trembling hands.

"I forgot to take a picture upstairs," he cried in a mournful tone. "I'll probably never have another chance to photograph a ghost."

"The ghost is gone," his wife snapped. "And so am I."

I held the gate politely for her as she fled, collected my wayward friend, and chivied him through the field and over the rotting fence. We were the last ones to reach the parked cars at the bottom of the mountain trail.

The last few days of our vacation were carefree, which was a relief. Our group had had enough supernatural occurrences to last a lifetime.

I got a phone call from Al shortly after we returned home. "Would you come by my place after work?" he asked. His voice sounded strange.

"Sure," I replied. I asked him why, but he refused to answer.

When I arrived at Al's place that evening, he ushered me into his dining room, sat me down at the table, and handed me an envelope full of developed pictures. I was puzzled. Had he invited me over to show me the Maine vacation photos? He could have brought them to Thursday poker night so everyone could look at them together, the way we always did after a shared vacation.

Al waved impatiently at me, not speaking, so I opened the envelope and went through the photos one by one. They were very good, as expected. Al took professional quality images. We had several of his pictures hanging on our walls at home.

A shiver ran through me when I reached the images of our haunted trek up the mountain. There were the trail and the overgrown field. The initial shot of the dilapidated farmhouse was very spooky, even in the sunlight. Here were the downstairs rooms, just as grimy and ruined as I remembered them. Al had even taken a photo of the hole he'd made when he fell through the floor. And there was the creepy staircase. Next came the room with the broken glass, followed by a rather cloudy photo of the locked seaman's chest. Then I flipped to the next photograph and gasped. It was the picture Al had taken of the haunted farmhouse, after everyone ran outside to escape from the ghost. Hovering between the creaking gate and the farmhouse was the translucent image of a woman, her form crackling with spectral white energy. A malicious grin was upon her lips and her eyes brimmed with vengeance. The ruined building could clearly be seen behind the figure, the gaping dark hole of the front door centered on her neck.

I dropped the picture and stared in dismay at Al. "She wasn't there," I gasped. "I watched you take the photo and no . . . one . . . was . . . there!"

Al nodded solemnly.

"I am never going ghost-hunting again," I declared.

"Me neither," said Al.

Death Light

CAPE ELIZABETH

Dear Emma,

The evening light's slowly fading through the windowpane. I reckon by the time the sun goes down, I will be dead and good riddance to me. You've thought me dead all these long years, wife, and so this letter will come as a shock to you. But I owe you an explanation for my behavior, and this is my last chance to confess. I've done you wrong twice, wife. Leaving you to think I was dead was the second wrong. The first wrong I did you was far worse.

I've loved your beautiful self just about forever, Emma. I followed you around the schoolyard when we were children, and when we grew up a bit I'd sit in my boat fishing and dream about taking you to the local dances and maybe sweeping you off your feet. You were in my thoughts every moment of every day, but I was too shy to tell you how I felt. I was just a poor fisherman's boy, and you were the gruff harbormaster's only daughter.

It was only after your pa died in a storm that I felt as if things became equal between us. I started calling on you twice a week, steady as can be. I was just one of many local boys who were buzzing around your widowed ma's place in those

DEATH LIGHT

days, but I thought I was your favorite. We could always laugh together, and I thought that was a good sign.

Then one day I was walking up the shore from my boat with a mess of cod I'd caught for you and your widowed ma, and I saw you leaning against the trunk of a big old fir tree in the side yard kissing Jack Welsh. Right then and there, the bottom dropped out of my world. I knew Jack was courting you, but I never dreamed you would like him better than me.

Love does funny things to a body. After that day, every time I saw Jack Welsh the world got red around the edges and I could barely breathe. I hated him so fiercely I wished him dead and crawling with maggots six feet under the churchyard. I cursed him every morning when I rose and every night when I went to bed. And every hour in between.

Late one evening at the dark of the moon, I saw Welsh alone beside his boat pulling in one of his crab traps. The whole world went red and dark around the edges. I trembled with rage, remembering the kiss beside the old fir tree. I grabbed a big chunk of driftwood that had swept up against a rock, crept up behind him, and hit him over the head. With a grunt, Welsh fell facedown into the lapping waves, his skull crushed and blood flowing into the water. I brought my boat to the spot where he lay partially submerged, dragged him in, and sailed out into the night-darkened bay to dump his body into the ocean. Good riddance.

It was a nine days' wonder, the disappearance of Jack Welsh. You were pale and thin for a while after he vanished, but my frequent visits and gifts eventually put the smile back on your face. We got married on the anniversary of Jack Welsh's death, though you can be sure I never shared that tidbit with you.

We were on our way down to Boston for our honeymoon trip on that first anniversary, so we didn't see the death light that appeared out in the bay, sailed over to the dock where Welsh kept his boat, and then floated to your ma's place to hover over the tree where I saw you kissing Jack. It vanished with a grunt, the sound a dying man might make after he was hit over the head with a piece of driftwood.

We moved in with your widowed ma when we came home from our honeymoon, and we were real happy that first year. Then one night I woke from a bad dream, and I swear I saw Jack's face pressed against our bedroom window, which looked out over the harbor. I gave a yelp that woke you up, and I had to make up an excuse for my jitters. It happened again the next night and then the next. It didn't stop until we traded bedrooms with your ma, since her window faced inland.

A week later, the death light made its second annual appearance in the center of the bay, paused on the shore where Jack died, and then came to hover over our house. Everyone in the settlement saw it. I felt as if I was wearing a brand that said "murderer." I was determined to move out of that haunted house. Fortunately, you and your ma were so frightened by the death light that neither of you objected when I put the house up for sale the next day and moved us into a nice cottage on the far side of the inlet by the end of the week.

As if triggered by our move, the death light started appearing once a month at the dark of the moon. It popped into existence right over the place where I dumped Jack's body into the ocean, flew to the place where I hit him with the driftwood, and then made its way to the old house where we'd lived with your ma. I felt as if the death light was looking for me, trying to figure out where I'd gone.

Everyone in our little community started talking about the mysterious light, which made me real nervous. Folks in the mercantile thought it might be your dead pa come back to visit his old home, or maybe some other seafaring friend who wanted to look in on you and your ma and didn't know you moved. The speculation was getting too close for my comfort. Every time the death light was mentioned, I pictured Jack bending over the crab trap and heard the grunt he made as he died.

After that, I made double and triple sure that I got home from fishing early enough to avoid any encounter with the death light. I didn't want Jack to find me again.

In August the Anderson boys and I got caught in a thick fog that prevented us from making it to shore before dark. It was very late when we pulled in. The fog swirled across the wharf and blotted out the dark sky as we tied up the boat. Suddenly the mist split in two around us, leaving a strange open channel between our boat and the center of the bay. On either side of the channel, fog billowed and swirled in huge gray walls. Within the empty space, the dark ocean reflected thousands of stars back at the night sky.

Then the death light appeared in the middle of the cleared-out channel. It was an eerie blue-white ball of fire that reflected blindingly off the walls of fog on either side. The death light came hurtling toward the three of us. The Anderson boys yelped with fear and flopped facedown on the wharf. I threw myself back into the boat and crouched in the bottom with my arms protectively over my head as the light honed in on my position. The ghost light darted around the boat, bouncing off the rigging. I swear I felt my hair sizzle as it hovered over my head. I refused to look up. As the eerie light pressed down on me, I saw Jack's dead face in my mind. It was dripping with blood from the terrible crushed skull. I heard the dying grunt he made as he fell.

After a moment, the light rushed away from me. I uncurled my trembling body and lunged for the side of the boat to see where it went. The death light hovered over the place where I'd murdered Jack, several hundred yards down the shore. I watched it float toward your ma's old home like it always did. Then it paused and changed direction. My heart nearly stopped when the death light came to rest over the roof of our new cottage. Jack Welsh may as well have hung a sign on our front door: "My murderer lives here."

The Anderson boys were still trembling facedown on the wharf and didn't notice where the death light had gone. But someone in the community was bound to notice and ask questions.

As soon as the death light vanished, I hightailed it home, packed a bag, and left. You asked me where I was going, but I couldn't tell you. I didn't know myself. You wanted to know when I'd be home, and I couldn't tell you that either. I just knew I had to go right away. Sooner or later, someone would figure out what that death light meant if I stuck around.

Dawn was breaking as I looked my last on our little house by the shore. A white figure stood by the gate watching my departure. It was the ghost of Jack Welsh. I knew then that I would never return. Jack had won you after all.

Your repentant husband,
Tom Wright

10

A Strange Encounter

MACHIASPORT

The day was dark and gloomy as we made our way south on Route 1, heading toward Acadia National Park.

"Looks like we are going to get some rain," my husband remarked from the driver's seat. "It's about time."

This was true, and I was happy that our drought might be over at last. Still, I liked fair, sunny weather, particularly for our fall leaf-peeping getaway. The menacing clouds and heavy atmosphere did nothing to uplift my spirits, although it did make the yellow leaves stand out against the gloom.

My husband of thirty years knew me well. A single glance had told him I was feeling a bit down, so he said: "You know what? We should get some fresh air. We are almost to Machiasport. Let's go down to Jasper Beach. You've always wanted to visit. That will cheer you right up."

My face lit up at the suggestion. I had been hankering for a visit since I first heard about Jasper Beach, but we never seemed to have the time. Harbor Cove, the inlet where the beach was located, was filled with billions of small- to medium-sized stones that formed a mile-long beach along the shore. The beach was classified as a barrier split, starting at an eroding bluff and

A STRANGE ENCOUNTER

ending at a tidal inlet. What fascinated me were the descriptions I'd read online about the sound the ocean waves made as they washed through billions of small stones. One traveler called it "magical," and I longed to hear it for myself.

My best friend, who grew up in Machiasport, told me there were a couple of supernatural stories associated with Jasper Beach that her school friends liked to tell around Halloween. One tale spoke of a young woman who perished somewhere along that stretch of the shoreline. Her phantom was said to wail in despair as she traversed the stony beach on foggy nights. Another story described the spirit of an evil man whose infamous deeds condemned him to roam the billions of stones in the inlet for eternity. I discounted the stories as fodder for the campfire. I was a scientific person and only believed what I could see and hear for myself. But my friend swore they were true.

The road leading to Machiasport had many twists and turns, but it also had spectacular views of the water in several spots. Even in the drizzling rain, the fall colors were so beautiful that I wanted to stop and take pictures, but my husband told me to make a note of interesting locations, and we'd pause on our way back to Route 1.

A half mile from Jasper Beach, the heavens opened, and rain pounded down on the roof of the car. The windshield wipers made frantic noises in their attempt to clear away the water, and Jim slowed to a crawl, particularly when we found ourselves at the top of a steep incline. The sign for the beach was directly at the bottom. I'd have been nervous trying to get into the entry in fair weather. In foul. . . . Well, I was very glad my husband was such a good driver, that's all I'll say.

After finding a parking place in an unpaved lot surrounded by rose bushes and sea grass, we pulled on our raincoats, grabbed two umbrellas, and ventured into the downpour. A happy woman in a yellow slicker entered the parking lot from a short trail and greeted us like long lost friends. We chatted about the beach as she put away her belongings and got into the car. "Have fun," she called as she pulled away.

The map called this place a beach, but after walking a couple of yards along the trail, what I spied was an enormous mound of small- to medium-sized stones. I stopped with my jaw agape. This wasn't at all what I'd expected. I thought I'd be looking down upon a craggy coastline, similar to the rest of Maine. Instead, I was gazing up at an enormous pile of smooth, fist-sized stones. If every landscaping company in the state of Maine decided to pile up their decorative small stones into one place, it would look exactly like this cove.

The stone-filled mound that was Jasper Beach stretched in a long crescent shape to either side of me, following the edges of a small cove. The rain-slick stones were of every size, shape, and color imaginable, some almost as big as my fist and others that could easily fit in the palm of my hand. Every last one of them had been rolled and polished by the sea before being deposited on this mound.

The billions of small stones lying before me made for treacherous footing. I wasn't sure if I could climb the mound without twisting my ankle, which I had injured playing pickleball a few weeks ago. Jim frowned at the conundrum that was Jasper Beach, then he furled his umbrella, ducked under mine, and offered me his hand for support. We made our way slowly up the mound, slippery wet rocks shifting beneath us with every footfall.

When we reached the top, the waters of the cove stretched before us, framed by a crescent of small rocks which cascaded down several levels to the ocean below. It was a beautiful sight, even with rain pounding steadily on the top of the umbrella and fog creeping in from both sides. And the sound made by the water was even more lovely than I had imagined. Large waves, chased inland by the windy cloudburst, swirled and clinked and washed through millions of stones in a manner that soothed the heart and mind. I could listen to that sound for hours. I took a deep breath of rain-soaked air and basked in my surroundings.

As I looked around, I realized we had the rocky beach to ourselves. No one else wanted to be out in such a downpour. A long, weathered log lay on my left, and more of the pebbled pile stretched to my right, past a small field with a house at the far end. What a lovely place.

The footing was too treacherous for me to walk without re-injuring my ankle, so I sat down on the driftwood and told Jim to explore without me. He gave me a kiss, put up the second umbrella, and set off toward the bluff, pausing occasionally to snap a photo with his phone. I watched him fondly for a moment, then shifted to look toward the beach lining the small field. The fog had thickened, obliterating the house from view. Billions of coastal stones vanished into the mist, while the wind murmured, the rain made soft tapping sounds on my umbrella, and the waves sighed as they washed through small rocks. I took several pictures, then set the camera in my lap. The sights and sounds were hypnotic, I thought. It felt almost like a meditation ceremony.

I don't know how long I sat listening to the waves when I heard someone wailing out in the fog. A cold breeze swirled under my umbrella, jolting me to attention. The fog was all around me, twisting in strange shapes. The sigh of the sea through small stones sounded mournful rather than soothing. Goose bumps ran down my spine when I saw a figure in the mist coming toward me from the direction of the farmhouse. It was a young woman, tall and pale, with flowing dark hair and a long dress that swirled in strange patterns as she walked. She was partially obscured by the fog, but I could see she was weeping, her face twisted with such despair that tears sprang to my own eyes. She needed someone to help her, I thought. No one suffering that much anguish should be left on their own.

I sat forward on the rough log, trying to find my footing among the slippery stones. I needed to speak with her, find out who she was and if she needed me to call for help. The girl was moving with surprising speed on the shifting stones. Faster even than Jim with his two healthy ankles. She trailed along the lower tier of stony beach, a few yards closer to shore than me. The mist seemed to cling to the girl, leeching the color from her skin and clothing, but her actions were clear enough. She was wringing her hands, and her steps would shortly take her into the waves if someone did not intercede. My heart leapt into my throat, and I lunged upward, the loose stones moving wildly underfoot. My ankle twisted and I fell back onto the log with a cry of pain.

Below me, the woman turned, and I saw to my amazement that she was floating a few inches above the stones. Our eyes met, and I was overwhelmed by the sudden flow of emotions that passed between us: pain, fear, loss, hopeless despair. I'd never felt such darkness in my life. My body drooped and tears streamed down my face. It was more than I could endure. Make it stop, I prayed desperately. Dear God, make it stop.

As if she sensed my agony, the phantom turned abruptly away, breaking eye contact. She stepped off the beach into the rain-drenched waves and vanished.

I screamed. I couldn't help it. It was too much for my overwrought senses.

I heard Jim's answering shout, and the sound of his feet stumbling over billions of rocks as he ran to my rescue. He tossed aside his umbrella as he knelt beside me. "What happened? Are you hurt? Is it your ankle?" he cried, leaning underneath my umbrella to look at my face.

I threw myself into his arms and sobbed out the whole story, the rain tapping its heavy rhyme on the umbrella overhead. The wind sprang up as I spoke, making the fog dance in strange patterns around us.

"I don't like this place," Jim said. "Let's get out of here."

Before I could protest, he furled the second umbrella and handed it to me. Then he swept me into his arms and carried me slowly across the rocky beach, choosing each footstep carefully among the slippery stones. When we reached the sandy dirt of the path, he set me down and checked my ankle.

"It is okay," I said. "A bit sore, but I can walk."

I demonstrated it by moving briskly down the path toward the parking lot. I was eager to get away from that haunted beach. I knew the memories I'd shared with that poor young ghost would stay with me for a very long time.

I was still shivering with cold and nerves when we reached the car. Jim opened the door, tucked me tenderly into the front seat, and took my umbrella to store in the trunk. A moment later, he slid into the driver's seat and turned on the heat to warm me up.

As he drove carefully out of the parking lot, windshield wipers working frantically against the downpour, Jim said: "I've had my fill of Jasper Beach. Next time, we will go straight to Acadia."

I fervently agreed.

The Sarah

FREEPORT

George Leverett fell in love with Sarah at first sight. The sun was shining on her hair, and her eyes were sparkling as she laughed at a joke made by one of the yardmen laying the keel of the new ship he and his partner had commissioned. He and Charles José would be hauling wood products and fresh fish to the West Indies in trade for sugar, rum, and coffee. George would captain the new vessel, and Charles would be his first mate. The young men were backed by George's father and Charles's uncle, and the financial outlook for their new enterprise was very good.

Charles José, as always, got in the first word with the lovely young woman. Over the following weeks, he pursued her with smooth vigor, his handsome face all smiles as he tried to win over her family. George was the quiet, dependable one in their partnership. He worshipped Sarah from afar, speaking little, eyes saying much.

As the new ship took shape, Sarah started singling out George at the shipyard, drawing him into conversation, inviting him to dine with her family, and sitting on the porch with him in the evening to watch the sunset. Her preference was

THE *SARAH*

obvious, and soon everyone in South Freeport was whispering of wedding bells.

Charles José was furious that the lovely girl had rejected him. When the partners were summoned to Portland to give a progress report to their financial backers, the two men argued the entire length of the trip. Charles was so incensed that he tried to push George and his horse over the side of the bridge in Yarmouth, hoping they would drown. But George kept his head and his seat and slipped past his would-be killer, galloping ahead to safety while the jealous Charles stewed in his rage.

Attempted murder was a step too far for George. He could understand a man's need to voice his displeasure with an unpleasant situation, but he needed a partner he could trust in a pinch, and that obviously was not Charles José. The two men ended their business partnership, and Charles left the city to start a new venture in the Caribbean.

When George returned to Freeport, he proposed to Sarah, and she joyfully accepted his hand. They planned to marry a few days after the official launch of the new ship, and Freeport was abuzz with excitement. Folks all over town eagerly speculated on every detail of the upcoming festivities, from Sarah's trousseau and wedding to the celebrations surrounding the new ship.

In September 1812, the new ship was launched into Freeport Harbor, to the cheers of all assembled. George beamed as he christened the ship. "She is called the *Sarah*," he said, winking at his bride-to-be. Her cheeks went pink with delight, and everyone applauded. The sun sparkling on the sea, the smell of brine and flowers in the air, the joyful noise of the crowd, and the love in the eyes of his betrothed forever encapsulated the moment in George's mind as one of the happiest in his life.

George woke at dawn on his wedding day, nerves a-jitter, and a sinking sensation in his stomach. The air was strangely still, as if a storm was brewing over the horizon. He frowned uneasily out of the window before turning his attention to the final wedding preparations.

They hit the first issue when they arrived at the church. With more than an hour to go before the wedding, the building was already overflowing with out-of-town guests. The locals from Freeport and surrounds were still on their way. George was hustled into a side room so he wouldn't catch sight of the bride when she arrived—which was bad luck—while the two families conferred. The father of the bride offered a large workroom at the shipyard as a new venue for the wedding, and everyone hurried over to prepare the space for a wedding and reception. The bride and groom went to separate locations to wait while several cousins redirected the guests.

When George's father stopped by with refreshments, there was more bad news. The preacher was ill and could not perform the ceremony. Sarah's brother was on his way to Yarmouth to ask their reverend to take his place. The wedding would have to be delayed until the evening. George nodded gravely, avoiding his father's eyes. Sailors were a superstitious lot, and he knew the setback on his wedding day would be taken as a bad omen.

Still, when George entered the workroom that evening, it was like walking into a storybook. The room was decorated with flowers and white cloth and candles. Benches with fine decorations were arranged before an altar, where the Yarmouth preacher stood holding his Bible. And the far end of the wedding hall was set up with tables already brimming with fine dinnerware and food.

The wedding guests smiled as George took his place before the altar. When his beautiful bride appeared on the arm of her father, George forgot to breathe. All he could see was his Sarah. George was overwhelmed with love and a deep sense of responsibility. He would take care of his lovely wife to the very best of his ability, for better or for worse.

When George and Sarah returned from their wedding journey, they realized that their troubles had just begun. Word of George's argumentative split with his business partner had spread far and wide. Coupled with the rumors of ill luck that hung over their wedding day, the Freeport sailors were reluctant to crew his new ship. George had to hire Portland men as officers, and they recruited sailors from Harpswell and other ports around Casco Bay.

Once he had a full complement, George set sail for Portland, where the *Sarah* would pick up its cargo for the Caribbean. He brought his wife and her mother along on the short voyage, wishing to spend a few more days with them before he departed for the West Indies.

Shortly after the *Sarah* left the harbor, the lookout spotted a three-masted, black-painted bark lurking offshore. It had no flag, and none of the seamen aboard were familiar with it. Captain and crew eyed the menacing bark with suspicion as they set sail for Portland, but there was little they could do beyond staying on alert. The ship trailed the *Sarah* all the way into Portland waters and docked nearby.

When George inquired about the bark, the harbormaster told him the vessel belonged to Charles José, his former business partner. Charles found the ship abandoned on a reef and brought it to Cuba for repairs. He christened the vessel the *Don Pedro Salazar* and hired an all-Cuban crew. He had recently sailed the bark into Portland harbor and registered it at his home port.

"A more rag-tag bunch of sailors never set foot in Portland," the harbormaster opined. "I'd keep a close eye on your women-folk, if you catch my meaning."

A shiver ran down George's spine. He wouldn't trust Charles within a mile of his lovely wife, or anyone in her family. He nodded his thanks to the harbormaster and hurried out of the office, his mind ablaze. His wife and mother-in-law were booked on the packet boat for the return voyage to Freeport, once the *Sarah* set sail for the West Indies. Keeping those reservations on the official books as a decoy, George went secretly to the stagecoach office and bought tickets for his wife and mother-in-law, along with a soldier he hired to guard their return journey.

George said his private goodbye to his wife the night before he set sail. "Come home to me," Sarah begged softly, her lip trembling slightly. "Always," George promised.

Sarah watched proudly from the dock as George, resplendent in his captain's uniform, strode aboard his ship and gave the order to depart. She didn't break down until the ship was out of sight, and only her mother could see her loneliness and fear. "He will be fine," her mother said, guiding her quickly over to their guard, who helped them aboard the stagecoach. "George is a good man and a careful captain. All will be well."

Sarah's father was late for dinner that evening. The owner of the shipyard had a troubled look in his eyes when he sat down to eat, and over supper he had a strange story to tell. "You know the packet boat you booked passage on?" he asked his wife and daughter as they ate their meal. "One of the sailors came to tell me that they were stopped and boarded by several rough men in a whaleboat. The strangers asked after you, Sarah. They said you should be turned over to them immediately. When the crew told them you weren't aboard, they tore apart the whole boat looking for you."

Sarah gasped and exchanged a worried glance with her mother.

"They made a mess of the packet boat," her father continued. "They searched every nook and cranny. When the men realized you weren't aboard, they cursed the crew and jumped back into the whaleboat and rowed away. The captain of the packet boat notified the authorities about the raid, and everyone sailing in or out of Freeport is on the lookout for those scalawags, though I doubt they will find them. I think they are already aboard a fast ship, heading for parts unknown."

"Do you think they are from the *Don Pedro Salazar*?" Sarah asked quietly.

Her father nodded. "I do. And I also think you are overdue for a visit to your sister. At least until things settle down here in Freeport."

Sarah nodded her assent and sent up a little prayer for her new husband, somewhere out on the sea with his enemy not far behind.

Aboard the *Sarah*, Captain George Leverett quickly became aware that his ship had a shadow. They were making good time down the eastern seaboard toward the Bahamas, but every watch the report was the same. A black-painted bark was always on the horizon, out of sight of everyone but the lookout. It trailed their ship like a ghost, and the crew grew more nervous and short-tempered with each passing day.

"We have to report it," the mate quietly urged his captain. "The men are afraid. I am afraid. I believe the crew will mutiny if we do not act."

"Then let us act," George said grimly. "Set a course for Nassau. We will report this aggressive behavior to the British Admiralty this very day."

When the order was given, the crew cheered and leapt to obey, eager to seek refuge and reinforcement in the closest harbor. As soon as the ship changed course, the *Don Pedro Salazar* hoisted her flag and set her sails for maximum speed.

"It's the Jolly Roger," the lookout shouted. "They've raised the skull and crossbones."

The bark was heavier than the *Sarah* and it gained swiftly on the fleeing ship. Badly damaged by cannon fire, the *Sarah* was swarmed by the pirate crew, who looted her cargo and killed the crew. Soon all but the captain lay dead upon the boards.

Captain Charles José ordered his crew to lash George to the mainmast and tie down the helm so the ship would sail out to sea. Once the stolen cargo was safely aboard the *Don Pedro Salazar*, Charles kicked his former business partner in the ribs and leaned down to whisper in his ear. "Sarah will forget you ever existed once she is my wife," he purred. Then he boarded his pirate ship and sailed away, leaving the *Sarah* and her dead crew to drift aimlessly on the wide ocean.

George was barely conscious when the pirates lashed him to the mainmast. He had fought to the bitter end, trying to save his crew, but they were overwhelmed. He heard Charles's final words, but they barely registered through the waves of pain coursing through his body. He dozed fitfully as the sun slowly fell across the horizon and the night rolled in.

A subtle shift in the direction of the ship awakened George from his stupor. He opened salt-crusted eyelids and looked upon a moonlit night. Around him, the dead bodies of his crew were rising and making their way to their assigned positions. All was silent, save for the whistle of the wind and the lap of the waves against the hull. George watched the first mate cut the lashings on the wheel and take his position at the helm. Bloodstained sailors mounted the rigging and adjusted the sails. The lookout, who had a wooden splinter through his forehead, climbed to his position, spyglass in hand. Not a word was spoken, but the crew performed their tasks with practiced ease. Judging by the stars, George saw that the first mate had turned the ship on a northward course. Dead or alive, the crew of the *Sarah* was sailing for home.

The ship's cook, a swarthy man with bloodstained clothes and a ghastly slit across his jugular, brought the captain a cup of water. He held it gently to George's lips and silently urged him to swallow. Then he cut the restraints and carried his captain to a sheltered place where the sun could not reach him before retreating to the hold. George watched his grisly crew with heavy eyes and nodding head. He fell asleep long before dawn.

Several weeks later, a square-rigger limped past several Harpswell fishermen, making its way through the channel between Potts Point and Haskell Island. The ship was battered almost past recognition: sails torn to shreds, hull nearly obliterated in places by cannon shot, and superstructure collapsed. Barely afloat, she still made good speed in the stiff breeze. A deathly pale figure stood at the helm, navigating expertly through the passage, but no other crew was visible.

The ship dropped anchor at Potts Harbor, and the crew members appeared out of thin air, lowering the single remaining lifeboat and rowing for land. The bloodstained first mate carried his captain ashore, laying his battered body gently upon a grassy knoll with the ship's log beside him. The crew saluted their captain and then faded back toward the lifeboat. As they rowed toward the ship, a low fog swirled in from the sea, obscuring everything from view. When it cleared, the *Sarah* was gone.

The stunned fishermen hastened through the mist to the lone figure on the shore, and George was taken to a nearby home to rest and recover. The last entry in the logbook documented the course change to Nassau, and George told his rescuers that he remembered being boarded by pirates, but nothing that happened afterward.

He gave a private account of the battle to his family when they were reunited, but only his wife—and later his children—heard the full version of events.

George Leverett lived happily to a ripe old age with his wife Sarah, but he never set foot on a sailing vessel again. He made no comment upon reports of a phantom vessel that made its way past Harpswell and into the harbor on nights when the fog swept in from the sea. Though sometimes he and Sarah walked down to the shore to watch for the battered square-rigger and wave to the phantom crew that saved George's life.

12

Playing Piano

PHIPPSBURG

Dah-dah-dum-dum-BLAT!

Charlie winced when his wife hit the wrong note on the piano for the thirty-second time that day. He knew it was the thirty-second time because he'd kept count as he went about his daily chores: cleaning the lighthouse, checking the supplies, mending the rowboat.

Charlie and his wife, Myrtle, lived on a small island off the coast of Maine. Charlie was the lighthouse keeper, and he worked hard to keep everything up-to-date, spankin' clean, and in perfect order. No ships were going to wreck on the local reef while he was in command of the lighthouse. Myrtle kept house and made crafts to sell at the local onshore market during their once-a-month trip into town.

Charlie and Myrtle had been married for almost ten years, and generally got along quite happily together, despite having no children. After she lost the first two, the doctor had told Myrtle that she wouldn't be able to have any more. Myrtle had taken the news stoically and had refused to adopt a child from the orphanage when Charlie proposed the idea. Still, Charlie

PLAYING PIANO

suspected she really did feel the lack of motherhood in her life, and that it was probably the cause of her latest obsession.

Charlie blamed himself, really. He should never have taken Myrtle to attend the concert when that highfalutin concert pianist came to town. But it was a special occasion, and everyone they knew was going. So Charlie and Myrtle went too. And Myrtle decided right then and there that what she wanted more than life itself was to play the piano.

Charlie tried to talk her out of it. No one in Myrtle's family was any good at music. Couldn't carry a tune in a bucket, the lot of them. In fact, when her Uncle Teddy played the fiddle, he cleared out the whole house. Even the neighbors went to town to escape the sound. Besides, Charlie argued, they couldn't possibly afford a piano. And how would they get it out to the island? Where would they fit one inside their small lighthouse?

But Myrtle was as stubborn as her Uncle Teddy. If she couldn't find a dad-gum way, she'd make one! Before Charlie could count to ten she'd bought a cheap, used piano (that was always out of tune) and hauled it over to the island on her brother Jamie's fishing boat. She would have kept it at the foot of their bed if Charlie hadn't drawn the line there. So Myrtle put Charlie's favorite rocking chair and table out in the woodshed and installed her piano in the main living space.

From that day on, it was practice, practice, practice. Morning, noon, and night Myrtle sat at the piano with her songbook open, plunking away at the keys. At first, there was not much to hear, and Charlie could ignore the sour sounds. But after a few months, she got better . . . and a lot worse. There were parts of her song that sounded pretty good; but she never, ever got that one line right. *Dah-dah-dum-dum-BLAT* went the piano, every time. Twelve weeks in a row she'd been playing the same song without any improvement. Sometimes she'd continue after the first *BLAT*, and that was even worse. *Dum-dum-BLAT-BLAT-ding!*

There was nowhere on the small island that Charlie could go to get away from the sound, even when he sat in his favorite rocker out in the woodshed with cotton in his ears. Myrtle's new hobby was the source of much contention between husband and wife, who had never argued before. Now they argued every day.

"At least try to learn another song," Charlie begged his wife. But Myrtle was stubborn.

"I ain't going to learn another song until I've mastered this one. You've got to practice to get better, Charlie."

"Your Uncle Teddy practices his fiddle every Saturday night," Charlie snapped, "and he hasn't gotten any better in fifty years."

But Myrtle refused to listen. She just went back to her piano and started playing again. *Dah-dah-dum-dum-BLAT / Dum-dum-BLAT-BLAT-ding.* Charlie went upstairs to polish the light. He put wax in his ears, but even that did not completely muffle the sound.

Things came to a head the day a nor'easter roared down on the island. Charlie and Myrtle were holed up together in the lighthouse hour after hour after hour. Charlie's chores were swiftly completed, and aside from regular checks on the light and a quick sweep of the beaches to make sure no ships were in danger, Charlie had nothing to do but sit and carve decoy ducks. And Myrtle played the piano. Hour after hour after hour. *Dah-dah-dum-dum-BLAT / Dum-dum-BLAT-BLAT-ding.*

Around 4:00 p.m. Charlie leapt to his feet and shouted at his wife to stop playing the blasted song. Myrtle leapt to her feet and shouted that she was going to practice until she got it right. After a brief but fierce argument, Myrtle sat down at the piano and started playing again. *Dah-dah-dum-dum-BLAT / Dum-dum-BLAT-BLAT-ding.*

Then something in Charlie snapped.

A little while later, he felt bad about the way he had chopped up the piano with his ax. After all, it was a valuable instrument. Try as he might, though, he couldn't feel bad about doing the same to Myrtle.

Charlie put on his oilskins, took up a shovel, and dug a grave out back of the woodshed. He buried all the little pieces of Myrtle with all the little pieces of her piano. He figured she would have wanted it that way. Later that night, with the nor'easter raging and pounding the island, and the lighthouse rattling and shaking wildly in the blast, Charlie got the best sleep he'd had in months. No more piano playing, ever.

The nor'easter blew itself out sometime the next morning. The island was peaceful and quiet once again, with no music at all save for the lap of the waves and the soughing of the wind through the pine trees. Charlie spent the rest of the day cleaning the blood off the floor and walls of the lighthouse. After that, he did his daily duties, moved his favorite rocking chair and table back into the main room, and carefully noted in the logbook the terrible tragedy that had befallen his wife during the storm.

Myrtle, according to the log, had been swept out to sea by a huge wave while heroically patrolling the beaches, helping Charlie look for shipwrecks.

In the middle of the night, Charlie was startled awake by a familiar sound. *Dah-dah-dum-dum-BLAT / Dum-dum-BLAT-BLAT-ding.* He sat bolt upright with an oath. It sounded just like Myrtle playing on the piano. But that was impossible—she was buried behind the woodshed!

Charlie leapt out of bed and felt around for his ax. Blast! He must have left it in the woodshed. He picked up a large piece of firewood and carefully stepped through the door into the main room, while the piano played its sour tune again and again. Charlie stared in astonishment at the glowing green translucent piano that stood once again in the place where Myrtle had put it. He could see his rocking chair and the end table right through the dad-blame instrument, which was somehow contriving to share space with them. The keys of the ghostly piano were playing all by themselves. *Dah-dah-dum-dum-BLAT / Dum-dum-BLAT-BLAT-ding.*

Then he heard Myrtle's voice coming from the stairway leading up to the light. "Charlie, over and over I told you . . . I ain't going to learn another song until I've mastered this one. You should have listened to me!"

Charlie whirled around and gazed toward the stairs. Standing a third of the way up the spiral staircase was the translucent white figure of his dead wife. And in her hands, she held his ax.

13

Turning the Tables

ANDROSCOGGIN COUNTY

When old Sam passed back just after the Civil War, he left a prosperous farm to his only son, who was an attorney. But the heir did not want the farm. Being a bookish fellow, he had gone to university and was now practicing law in Boston. There were two houses on the property, one for Sam and one he built for his elderly in-laws, who were now deceased. So, the heir decided to split the land into two separate properties and made a nice profit from the sale of each.

It was the division of the properties that started the problem. My father bought old Sam's place, and his archrival Jedediah bought the in-law's place. If the two men had ignored one another, things wouldn't have gotten so bad. But the best apple tree in the whole county stood right smack dab on the boundary line. If the surveyor had moved the property line one yard either way, there wouldn't have been an issue. But the property line went dead center through the middle of the tree, so said my father, and by rights the two men should split the harvest 50-50. Jedediah, on the other hand, claimed the property line went three-quarters of the way through the massive trunk, and thus he deserved three-quarters of the apples from the fabled tree.

TURNING THE TABLES

The two men argued over that apple tree every fall harvest for years. I have to say, the apples from that tree were worth fighting for. It was some kind of hybrid apple with a sweetly tart flavor that tasted divine in an apple pie. Mama called them Old Sam's after the former property owner. I don't know if the tree had a formal name. I never heard of one.

Things got nasty about a decade after they bought the properties. Jedediah accused Father of sneaking out in the middle of the night to harvest apples on the sly. He claimed the tree was several bushels short one morning when he went out to check on the fruit. The two men got into fisticuffs, since Father didn't like being called a thief or a liar. Farmhands from both sides had to pull them apart, and one of the men pointed out some overlooked bear tracks and half-eaten apples. Jedediah backed off but refused to apologize.

The next day, Father went to the authorities and asked them to send a surveyor to review the property line and officially pronounce on the position of the apple tree. When the survey came back in Father's favor (60 percent on our property, 40 percent on Jedediah's property) our neighbor raged for a week, loudly and publicly. His outcry grew so acerbic that the authorities sent a second survey team to recheck the boundary line. The second group said the property line divided the trunk in half, and the 50-50 split was officially recorded on the town books.

When Jedediah contested this second review, the town took steps. The authorities gave the feuding men two choices: The town could hire someone to harvest the tree each year and split the apples 50-50 between them, or one man must sell his portion of the apple tree to the other and relinquish his claim. Neither man would sell, so the town assigned a neutral party to pick the Old Sam apples annually, and they charged Father and Jedediah a handsome fee for his services.

Each year on Apple Man Day (as we called it), all work stopped on both farms. Father and Jedediah watched the town harvester like a hawk during the entire process, lest he trick them out of a single apple. Farmhands on both properties found excuses to work in the vicinity and placed bets on the final tally. Mrs. Jedediah, who was as sweet as her husband was sour, put her rocker in the shade of the barn and sat knitting while the apple count progressed. I would sit next to her, or perch on the fence the town erected between the two properties after all the fuss. Even Mama, who was appalled by the entire apple tree fiasco, made lemonade for everyone and laid it out on trays in the shade, though she never stayed to watch. Every single apple was counted, even those rotting on the ground. The Apple Man would split the very last apple down the middle with a knife in years when the tally was uneven so that the harvest was exactly 50-50.

Jedediah passed away suddenly the year I turned twenty. He had problems with his heart, and it failed him right there under the tree on Apple Man Day. It was the only time I heard Father speak kindly to his nemesis. I ran for the doctor, who lived two doors down, but Jedediah was too far gone and died just before supper.

Mrs. Jedediah asked her widowed niece to come live with her after her husband died. I picked up Anna and her baby boy at the train station, brought them home, and helped with their bags. Just to be neighborly, you understand. Anna's fisherman husband died at sea and had never gotten to meet her little son Clark. Which was a darn shame. The little chap had an engaging grin and just one tooth. Baby Clark loved the mush his young mama made for him using the Old Sam apples.

Anna was a quiet beauty that stole right into this fellow's heart. She was very interested in the spiritualist movement, so when I saw an announcement in the paper saying that a very famous medium was coming to the area, Anna wrote to invite her to stay at the farm and hold a séance. We were astonished and delighted when she wrote back in the affirmative.

Everyone in town wanted to see the famous Madam Holly. Mrs. Jedediah was aflutter with excitement. This would be the social event of the year. She and Anna decided to hold a dinner and séance with a select number of guests, followed by a public lecture and demonstration by Madam Holly afterwards. Everyone who wished could come and meet the medium.

Our family was invited to supper to welcome Madam Holly on the day she arrived. She was about Mama's age, plump and pretty with fancy, floaty garments the like of which I had never seen. And she wore a large turban on her head. She greeted

Anna with a kiss, cooed over baby Clark, and said to me: "You and I knew each other in another life."

The next day, while Madam Holly rested from her long journey, I pitched in with the setup of the barn. Mama took charge of baby Clark while Mrs. Jed and Anna cooked up a storm. Even Father came over with our farmhands to set up the tables and chairs in the now-pristine barn. We curtained off two sections of the barn: one for the meal and another for the séance. The rest of the space had been turned into the lecture hall, with long wooden benches we constructed for the occasion and a small stage built at the far end.

The dinner guests arrived shortly after we finished setting up. We filled every single chair at the dinner table, with Madam Holly presiding at the head and Mrs. Jedediah at the foot. We feasted on wild game, brown bread, beans, and greens, with wild blueberry pies to cap it off. Not one bite remained of that delicious supper.

We cleared the dishes in record time and ushered everyone into the smaller space we had prepared for the séance. Night had fallen while we ate, and the only light came from the candles the medium had requested. A fancy candelabra sat at the center of the round table. It was a special order just for this occasion, and Mrs. Jedediah was incredibly proud of it. The curtained area was quite dark, and the guests hushed immediately when Madam Holly stepped into the space. She was arrayed in robes even more magnificent than those of the previous evening. The turban added an impressive twelve inches to her height.

I sat down between Anna and my father. I have no idea why my pa decided to attend this portion of the evening. He always said séances were made-up nonsense whenever we read about them in the newspaper, but he decided to attend this one. He must have been curious.

"Let us begin," Madam Holly intoned. We all held hands as she called upon her spirit guide Tarsa, who she introduced as an ancient Persian fire priestess born two thousand years ago. She chanted in a language I did not understand until she was in a light trance, then passed her hands several times through the flaming candles in the candelabra. The guests gasped in amazement, for her skin was not burned by the fire. I lit the candles myself, so I knew this was a real demonstration of power and no trickery.

When she spoke next, Madam Holly's voice was husky and slightly deeper, with a slight accent that was quite different from her normal tones. I assumed it was the voice of Tarsa, her spirit guide, speaking through her.

"The spirits are here, and eager to speak with us," Madam Holly said. "Is there someone present with the initials E. J.?"

There was. Edgar Johnston gasped and said: "I am here."

"Very good," Madam Holly returned. "Your mother says you will find your lost pocket watch behind the dresser in the bedroom."

Edgar swallowed tears and said: "Thank you, Mama. Are you well?"

"Your mother is at peace in her heavenly home. She will see you again by and by," the medium replied. "Now, who among those gathered replies to the name Betty?" The woman across from me answered in the affirmative.

And so it went. For almost an hour, Madam Holly (or Tarsa, the spirit possessing her) called out names and initials or asked pointed questions about people or objects shown to her by the spirits, until nearly everyone at the table had spoken with a lost loved one.

Strangely, neither of our hostesses had been singled out by the medium, though they had each lost a spouse in the past year. I was not the only one who recognized this oversight. Beside me, Father stirred. When Madam Holly paused in her inquiries, Father said: “We haven’t heard yet from Jedediah. Surely, he has a message for his good wife?”

At his words, a strange expression crossed the face of the medium. Her lips hardened and her features appeared more rugged, almost masculine. When she replied, it was in the familiar baritone voice of Jedediah.

“You,” roared the spirit of our deceased neighbor, speaking directly through Madam Holly. “You brought in the authorities. You lost me those apples. Seventy-five percent of that tree was mine!”

The table under our clasped hands started trembling. Everyone gasped as it rose a few inches and lurched sideways, knocking my father in the chin. Father reeled backward, and his chair tipped over. He hit the floor with a bang and yelped in pain. A blaze of light shot out of Madam Holly’s body and hovered above her head. It took on the misty form of Jedediah. He swooped over the table, grabbed the fancy candelabra, and dove toward my father. With a shout of alarm, Father scrambled backwards on all fours, trying to squeeze under the curtain that we’d used to portion off the space from the rest of the barn. It caught on his belt buckle, and he dragged it down in his haste. Father’s drapery-swathed figure leapt upright and ran blindly for the door, Jed and his blazing candelabra right on his heels.

"Please excuse me," I said politely to Anna, Madam Holly, and the terrified guests. "I believe I am required elsewhere."

I raced out of the barn and saw my father running for the fence line, pursued by the outraged ghost. The curtain was still tangled around his body, hampering his progress, and parts of it were already aflame. The candelabra blazed with preternatural strength in the hands of the glowing phantom.

"Mr. Jedediah, if you aren't careful, you will set the apple tree on fire," I called breathlessly as I caught up with the unnatural pair.

Jed's ghost swung around to look at me. "Dag nab it, lad. You were always the sensible one in the family. I wish you were the owner of the farm, not that scallywag over there." He gestured toward Father, who had tripped over the edge of the curtain and fallen to the ground, where he frantically rolled about, trying to put out the fire.

"When I marry Anna, our two properties will become one farm again," I said. "If Anna agrees to my proposal, that is."

"I agree," a breathless voice said from behind me. Anna had followed me from the barn just in time to hear my proposal. She stepped forward and took my hand, claiming it and my heart as well.

The ghost beamed with approval and the candelabra blazed with joy. His smile faded somewhat when Anna glared at him. "Uncle Jed, you are in big trouble," she scolded. "You didn't speak to my aunt or even acknowledge her presence before you began berating our neighbor over those dad-blame apples. She was *heartbroken* by your oversight. I swear I will cut that tree down with my own two hands if you don't fix your error immediately. Aunt Jed is *crying* in the old cow stall!"

Anna looked so ferocious that the phantom floated backwards a pace. The candelabra extinguished abruptly, and he looked ashamed. "I'll take care of that," Jedediah said humbly to his niece. Turning toward me, he said: "You take good care of my niece and my apple tree, boy. Or I'll come back!"

The fancy candelabra dropped to the ground as the spirit sped like a shooting star back toward the barn. Anna picked it up and examined it for damage. Her aunt had paid a pretty penny for the piece.

I scooped up the burning, shrouded figure writhing on the ground, stalked over to the horse trough, and dumped him into the water. Father emerged sputtering with cold and indignation. "You had best go home before you cause more trouble," I said briskly, pulling him out of the trough and freeing him from the sodden drapery.

"Yes, son," he said meekly. Glancing behind me, he added: "Welcome to the family, young lady. I hope you like apples."

"I do," she replied, playfully shaking the candelabra at him. He laughed a little and hurried away.

The rest of the evening was a social triumph by anyone's standards. The dramatic end to the séance caused quite a stir among our neighbors. The preternatural source of my sudden betrothal would be discussed for years to come. Inside the barn, the dinner guests lined up to congratulate Anna and me, while outside the barn, carriages lined up along the lane as townsfolk arrived for the public portion of the evening.

The spiritualism lecture and demonstration were a resounding hit. Many people connected with old friends and family members that night. The demonstration ended with a standing ovation for Madam Holly and Tarsa, her spirit guide.

The medium was invited to return to our town whenever her travels brought her back this way.

Father was billed for the curtains he destroyed at the séance, as well as a replacement for the fancy candelabra the phantom used to set him on fire. Though he was loath to admit it, old Jedediah had finally turned the tables on Father and triumphed in the matter of the apple tree.

Anna and I married in the spring when the Old Sam apple tree was in bloom. Father deeded the portion of his property surrounding the tree to me and Anna as our wedding present. Mama welcomed Anna's baby son Clark into our family with open arms. She'd been hankering for a grandchild and now she had one. Mama helped Mrs. Jed watch over the baby while we were away on our wedding journey. When we returned, I moved into the Jedediah household and helped my new wife and Mrs. Jed run the farm. So, everything worked out just fine for all of us.

PART TWO

Powers of Darkness and Light

14

The Witch Bridle

KITTERY

Skipper Perkins was so tight with his money that you needed a chisel to pry it out of his fist. So when Old Betty Booker came to the dock early one morning and said, "Bring me a bit o' halibut, Skipper Perkins," his reply was short and to the point: "Show me your sixpence, ma'am, and I'll show you some fish."

This wasn't the most tactful answer to make to the local witch. Most of the other skippers made sure to slip Old Betty Booker a few haddock on the house whenever she came asking. But Skipper Perkins was so thrifty he would have charged the Good Lord himself if He'd come a-knockin' for some fish. So he certainly took no mind of Old Betty Booker, standing on the dock with an ill-bodin' scowl on her rugged face as she watched his ship sail away into the dawn while the wind blew her raggedy gray hair this way and that. Finally Old Betty Booker made a grasping motion with her hand, as if to capture the wind. Then she blew it away across her palm in the direction Skipper Perkins had taken his ship.

And from that moment, Skipper Perkins was plagued with bad luck. His men fell ill. A gale tore up his sails while the waves

THE WITCH BRIDLE

battered his ship up and down, and the fish wouldn't bite. He came home poorer than he left.

Soon after he got home, a rumor reached Skipper Perkins that shook him down to his skinflint core. Old Betty Booker was making a witch bridle out of horsehair, strands of tow, and the bark of yellow birch, and every bit of her bridle had Skipper Perkins's name on it. She was planning on riding Skipper Perkins like a horse, away down to York Harbor on a night of her choosing.

Well, Skipper Perkins got into quite a panic when he heard the news. He took to double-barrin' his door at night and making sure he was home before sunset. Not that these precautions kept him from shiverin' and shakin' all night long in fear of Old Betty Booker and her witch bridle. Then one morning a message came from Old Betty Booker. She was brewin' up a storm in her warming pan. When the storm was done, she would set it free, and during that storm she was going to ride Skipper Perkins down to York Harbor with her witch bridle.

The storm came right on schedule, a-howlin' and a-blowin' as fierce as ever it could be. The creek was a-floodin' and the wind nearly bendin' the trees in half. Inside their houses, people were huddled around damp fireplaces and prayin' that Old Betty Booker would not remember them that night.

As for Skipper Perkins, well, he was double-bolted inside his house and every movable piece of furniture he possessed was piled up against the door. Then he hid himself under the bed and waited for Old Betty Booker. The wind was shriekin' down the chimney and rattlin' against the windows, and the rain was beatin' on the roof so hard a body could hardly think for the noise of it. But through the almighty racket of the storm, Skipper Perkins could hear a devilish wailing that could only be Old Betty Booker.

"Bring me a bit o' halibut, Skipper Perkins."

The front door began rattlin', and he heard the sound of witch claws scratchin' on the walls. Slipping out from under the bed, Skipper Perkins rushed to push the furniture tighter against the rattlin' door.

"Bring me a bit o' halibut, Skipper Perkins," Old Betty Booker howled again. The gale seemed to rise up and howl with her. The door shook fiercely and began to open. Rain came pelting in, and Skipper Perkins could hear the chattering of the witches just outside. He kept pushing against the furniture in sheer panic, his bare feet sliding slowly back and back as the door opened.

Suddenly Skipper Perkins gave a yelp of terror and leapt for the bed. He dived under the covers, shakin' in fear. With the resistance gone, the door popped open and the witches came troopin' inside, led by Old Betty Booker, holding the witch bridle and a whip.

"Bring me a bit o' halibut, Skipper Perkins," she cackled, pulling him, covers and all, off the bed. Skipper Perkins stared up into her wild eyes, quaking in terror.

The witches stripped off his nightclothes and held him down as Old Betty Booker bridled him up. Then Old Betty Booker climbed up on his back, and the other witches climbed up on top of hers, and with a crack of the whip Skipper Perkins was trotting through the gale in a blind panic, heading for York Harbor.

The night was as wild as they come, but not nearly as wild as the witches riding atop Skipper Perkins. They cackled and shouted and cursed, and when he slowed, their witch claws bit into him, making him shriek and run faster. When he staggered into York Harbor, Old Betty Booker made Skipper Perkins turn 'round and take them back to Kittery.

It wasn't until the darkest hour, just before cockcrow, that Old Betty Booker released Skipper Perkins from the witch bridle. He collapsed next to his front door, more dead than alive, and lay looking up into her wild face, too tired to be frightened. She said: "Don't you go chargin' sixpence to a poor old woman no more, Skipper Perkins." Then Old Betty Booker and her witch-familiars vanished into the dark, and the storm went with them. Skipper Perkins crawled through his front door, past the mound of furniture, and curled up in the blankets, too worn to climb onto his bed.

For three weeks Skipper Perkins lay abed, nursin' his wounds and telling his story to the wonderin' neighbors. When he finally got up, the first thing he did was catch a mess of halibut and send them over to Old Betty Booker, free of charge.

15

Specter Moose

SHERMAN

I had some business over in Macwahoc one fine day in September 1900, which was a good twenty miles from Sherman. This put me into a bit of a quandary. I was taking charge of my brother's lumber camp for the season, and there was a lot of work to do before the cold set in. I was miffed at being called away, so when a buddy of mine offered his bicycle to help shorten the journey, I was quick to accept.

I hadn't been on a bicycle in a while, and I'd forgotten how much fun they could be. As soon as I was out of earshot, I whooped like a young'un and let her go on the first big downhill slope I encountered. It's a good thing the tough lumbermen I managed couldn't see me on my journey to Macwahoc. I acted as silly as any boy: riding on one wheel, sailing through the air over bumps, skidding around turns, chasing foxes off the road. I hadn't had so much fun in years.

When I concluded my business in Macwahoc, I went looking for my cousin, who worked nearby, hoping to have a quick bite to eat before the return journey. He invited me to take a meal with him at a local inn, since his missus was over at her sister's

SPECTER MOOSE

place. Over big bowls of clam chowder, he asked me if anyone had spotted the specter moose this autumn.

"The specter moose is just a myth," I said with a frown. I had no time for such nonsense. "The biggest moose I've ever seen weighed nine hundred pounds with an antler spread of four and a half feet. There is no such thing as a giant white moose. Someone made it up."

My cousin chuckled. "You tell that to John Ross," he said. John was a well-respected woodsman from Bangor. His reputation for honesty was undisputed.

"John Ross saw the specter moose?" I asked, wondering how I'd missed this juicy tidbit. "I thought it was just that taxidermist fellow and that man from Massachusetts. I read about them in the papers."

"Oh no! John was one of the first to see the specter moose way back in 1891, when he was traveling from between Big Lobster and Little Lobster with the camp foreman," Bobby said. "He told me all about it the last time he came through town."

"What did it look like," I asked, still not convinced that it wasn't a tall tale invented to pass the time during long nights in the lumber camps.

"John said it was fifteen feet tall, about twenty-five hundred pounds, and a grayish-white color," my cousin reported. "The antlers were about ten feet across, and he counted twenty points on each side."

"That's impossible," I said flatly.

"If it was one of the big game hunters who told me about a giant gray moose that was impervious to bullets and could vanish into thin air, I wouldn't have believed it," my cousin returned, calmly sipping his coffee. "But it was John who saw him. And he was telling the truth. I could tell."

We paused for a moment when the woman waiting tables came to take our dessert order. When we had two big portions of blueberry pie in front of us, I asked: "Where do you reckon it came from?"

"John thinks it came down out of Labrador or maybe even from British Columbia. Somewhere remote," my cousin replied after swallowing a mouthful of pie. "He says it's a wily old fellow with good hearing and an exceptional sense of smell."

"Or maybe it really is a specter," I joked. We both chuckled at this sally.

I took another bite of dessert and changed the subject: "This pie tastes pretty good, but I think your wife's pie is better." The conversation moved on to family matters, the specter moose forgotten.

I was replete and disinclined for exercise by the time we said our farewells. But I had to get back, and so I mounted the bicycle with less glee than before and began peddling back to Sherman.

I got my second wind about halfway home and started enjoying the ride. The foliage was turning, some reds and yellows already peeking through the green. And when I rounded a bend, I startled another small fox. My speeding bicycle and friendly whoop sent it scurrying away, but I caught another glimpse of him through the trees. He seemed to be trotting along a deer path parallel to the road, staying just out of my line of sight. I couldn't tell who was playing with whom, but I enjoyed the company.

Not long after, I reached a steep hill. Oh boy. The incline had been a lot of fun on the outgoing (and downward) journey, but I did not fancy going back up. I got off and started climbing, wheeling the bicycle beside me. I was in a bit of a puff by the time I reached the summit, so I paused at the top, leaning heavily against the handlebars as I regained my breath. I stared casually around and saw a big gray draft horse grazing on some bushes a few yards down the road. Its head was completely buried in the shrubbery, its enormous body blocking most of the lane. With that coloring, I reckoned it was a Percheron that had escaped from his pasture. The farmer must be getting a good stud fee from this horse. It was the biggest I'd ever seen.

Then the creature raised its head out of the bushes. Enormous antlers ten feet across with eighteen-inch velvet hands and one, two . . . twenty prongs on each side. John Ross's estimate of fifteen feet high and one and a quarter tons was spot-on, I realized, my breath catching in my throat. My cousin would be thrilled to hear the stories of the specter moose were true.

We gazed at one another for a moment, the specter moose and I. Then I noticed tell-tale warning signs from my previous moose encounters. His dark eyes were gleaming, his nostrils were tense, his gray-white shoulders had bunched up, and . . . was he lowering his antlered head? Yes, he was.

When the specter moose snorted and stomped his foot, I realized that this phantom was real—or at least really annoyed at my presence in its territory. I was going to be skewered on those enormous prongs. I yelped, dropped the bicycle, and scrambled for the woods.

The specter moose came barreling toward me like an express train, his rack so wide the antlers brushed the leaves on either side of the lane. I ran past the first tree I encountered. It was too thin and would bend down to the ground if I climbed it. I practically levitated myself up the second tree, but the branch broke under my weight, and I fell to the ground, convinced of my impending doom. The ground was shaking under the weight of those thundering hooves. Then I saw the third tree in the row. It was a fine large specimen that could easily hold its own against a charging moose. Or so I hoped. I scrambled upward with impressive speed until I was well hidden among the leaves.

The enormous gray-white moose slid to a stop beside the bicycle, planting his front hooves on either side of it. He sniffed and poked at the wheel suspiciously, huffing several times in bemusement as he examined this strange interloper. I held my breath, hoping the specter wouldn't stomp the bike to pieces. My buddy would not be happy.

Finally, the huge creature snorted, shook himself from antlered head to tail, his dewlap flapping merrily, then sped off into the woods, knocking over a group of saplings as if they were weeds. And just like that, he was gone. Vanished without a trace. Exactly what one should expect from a respectable specter.

I gasped and flopped back against the trunk of the tree. That was too close. My whole body started to shake, and my heart pounded so loudly I feared the return of the territorial specter should he hear it. Then I realized the wind was blowing toward me, so the moose probably could not smell me. So as long as I stayed quiet, I wouldn't be shaken off my limb by an annoyed specter with a rack that was longer than me.

I remained in that tree for a good ten minutes before I was convinced it was safe to come down. I think I broke bicycle-riding records on my speedy return to Sherman. Lord help, I *never* wanted to see the specter moose again. Though it made a good story, once I was recovered enough to tell it.

I kept my eyes and ears open after that, collecting stories about the gray moose. Each year, several hunters claimed to have shot it, though the beast was apparently impervious to bullets, for no one brought in a carcass. Reports of the specter moose's wanderings came from every wooded section of northern Maine, and sportsmen came from everywhere to shoot him. As one newspaper said: "The hunters get near enough to be frightened but stay too far away to get a good shot." That seemed about right.

My favorite newspaper tale described a skeptical sportsman-turned-photographer who encountered the specter moose near Chairback Mountain but forgot all about the camera in his hand until it was too late to get a picture of the beast.

One of the last credible sightings came in 1938, when a fellow saw the specter moose—or more probably one of his descendants—near Chesuncook Lake. He was watching a herd feeding in a large bog when he spotted three antlered males at the timberline. Two regular browns and a gray that made his companions look like miniatures. In an eyeblink, they faded away.

Was it a real moose or a specter I encountered that day? Whenever folks ask me that, I have a hard time answering. He acted like a real moose. But real moose aren't impervious to bullets. And they don't live for thirty-eight years. I still don't have a good answer.

But I do know two things for certain: Sightings of the specter moose have persisted for decades, and if the specter moose lowers his antlers at you, your best option is to run like the dickens and look for the nearest tree.

16

La Chasse Galerie

ST. JOHN VALLEY

Maman was none too pleased when not one, but both of her French-Canadian daughters married American men and moved across the border to Maine. My husband did not speak much French when we first met, but I gradually taught him. When Maman finally came to visit, he chattered to her like a native of Quebec, which pleased her greatly. As a reward, she told him many stories that she had learned as a child. Roger's favorite story was about *la chasse galerie*—the Flying Canoe.

"Long ago," Maman told Roger, "but not so long ago, there were a number of lonely lumbermen working in the center of a very large forest. They cut down mammoth trees and watched them crash into the thick snow in exactly the place where they said the trees would land. They would cut up the trees and haul them hither and thither. They worked hard, *mon Dieu*, very hard indeed! But the woodsmen were lonely for the women they had left behind."

Roger sat on a stool beside the kitchen counter, listening enthralled to the tale as Maman made dinner. Maman placed a cutting board and some carrots and celery in front of him, and

LA CHASSE GALERIE

he automatically started chopping them up for salad while she continued her story.

"On New Year's Day it snowed so hard no work could be done. The men huddled in their camp and spoke longingly of their home. They passed around the rum and drank toasts to the New Year, but finally a lumberman named Baptiste said what they were all thinking: 'I wish to go home today and see my girl!' There were murmurs of agreement, but Jean replied: 'How can we go home today? There are more than two meters of snow on the road, and more snow is falling. You are crazy, Baptiste.'"

"What happened next?" asked Roger, his eyes wide. Maman smiled at him and continued her tale.

"'Who said we were *walking* out of here?' asked Baptiste. 'I am going to paddle out in my canoe.'

"Now the men all knew that Baptiste had a canoe with paddles out back of the camp. The woodsman had made a pact with the devil in exchange for it. If Satan would make the canoe fly wherever Baptiste wished, the woodsman would not pray the Mass for an entire year. The devil made two restrictions on the deal. If Baptiste did not return the canoe before dawn, the devil could keep his soul. And while Baptiste was using *la chasse galerie*, he could not say the name of God, fly over a church, or touch any crosses, or the canoe would crash."

Maman paused to put something in the oven, and then said, "Many of the lumbermen refused to participate in Baptiste's New Year's scheme, but he managed to find seven companions to fly back home with him in the canoe to visit their women. Baptiste and his friends got into the canoe, and Baptiste pronounced the magic words: '*Caïdemór Lerricht! Caïdemór Lerricht! Caïdemór*

Lerricht!' When he was done binding himself to the devil, the canoe rose into the air and the men began to paddle their way homeward through the sky. Their womenfolk were so glad to see them! They celebrated long into the night, drinking and dancing. It was close to dawn when the men realized they had to return the canoe to the lumber camp by dawn or forfeit their souls.

"They searched for Baptiste and found him as drunk as a lord lying under a table at the inn. They bundled him into the canoe, spoke the magic words, and paddled away.

"Knowing that Baptiste would start swearing if they woke him, one of the men tied him up and gagged him so he would not speak the name of God at an inopportune moment and crash the canoe. When Baptiste awoke, he sat up, struggling with the ropes that bound him. He managed to loosen the gag and shouted, '*Mon Dieu*, why have you tied me up?' At the name of God, the canoe took a nosedive, plunging toward the ground. It hit the top of a large pine tree and broke apart. The lumbermen tumbled down, vanishing into the deep twilight that precedes the dawn. They were never seen again!"

Roger gave a sigh of delight. "What a marvelous story," he said, and kissed Maman on the cheek. Maman giggled and blushed like a schoolgirl.

Not long after Maman returned home, Roger went to Quebec City to take a summer class in preparation for a new business certification. If he passed the class, his company would significantly raise his salary. This was excellent news for our family, since we were expecting our first child and could use the money. But I was just five weeks shy of my delivery date, and Roger was nervous about leaving me alone so close to my time. So, my sister and her husband volunteered to stay with me at our fishing camp on the lake until his return. It would calm my husband's fears and make a nice vacation for them.

Béatrice and Phillip spent their time boating and swimming and fishing on the lake when they weren't busy pampering me. Béatrice cooked special meals to tempt my appetite, and Phillip set up a comfortable seat for me out in the backyard, where I could put up my feet and look out over the water. Roger phoned each evening, and he told me about his class and how many folks mistook him for a native of Quebec.

Our peaceful sojourn was dispelled suddenly when I went into labor three weeks early. The contractions were ten minutes apart, and the doctor told me to stay at the camp until they were closer to five minutes. I was distraught. Roger was still in Quebec, and I was convinced he would not make it to Maine in time to see our baby born. When I called and told him the news, he promised to drive home as fast as he could.

I sat outside with Béatrice, trying to stay as relaxed as I could between labor pains. My contractions were only eight minutes apart when Roger phoned from a north country tavern to tell me the car had broken down. I tried to be brave, knowing Roger felt terrible about missing the birth of our son, but I couldn't help crying. I hung up slowly and went back outside to walk up and down the yard, hoping that the walking would make the baby come faster.

About an hour later, as I sat in my comfortable chair sipping water and trying to ignore the contractions, which continued steadily at eight minutes, I caught sight of something flying low over the horizon. I didn't hear an engine, and the shape of the object was unlike any seaplane I had ever seen.

"What is that?" I asked Béatrice. She shaded her eyes and then went inside to get her binoculars. She focused on the object for a moment and then dropped the binoculars in shock.

"It is *la chasse galerie*!" she cried. "And Roger is inside it with seven other men!"

"What!" I cried, snatching up the binoculars from the ground and focusing them on the flying object. She was right. Roger was sitting in a flying canoe, paddling as fast as he could. He was accompanied by seven seedy characters who looked as if most of their lives had been spent in bars. As *la chasse galerie* sailed toward us above the lake, Roger spotted Béatrice and me standing on the lawn.

"*Mon Dieu,* Cosette!" he shouted. "Shouldn't you be at the hospital?"

At the name of God, the canoe shuddered to a halt and then tipped forward, dumping Roger out the front end. He plunged into the lake and came up sputtering with indignation. The men in the boat laughed uproariously at Roger and then grabbed their paddles and began chanting some strange words that sounded ominously close to those Maman had used in her story. The canoe began flying forward again, and *la chasse galerie* disappeared over the treetops.

Roger swam to shore as fast as he could and stumbled, dripping and swearing, onto the dock just as Phillip came outside to find out what all the shouting was about.

"Good lord, Roger, where did you drop from?" Phillip asked in astonishment. Béatrice and I burst out laughing. Roger made a growling noise and came up to me. "Why aren't you at the hospital?" he demanded in a grumpy tone.

"Because the contractions are still eight minutes apart," I explained soothingly.

"The doctor doesn't want Cosette to come in until the contractions are five minutes apart," Béatrice explained as I tried to breathe through another contraction.

"We'd best get you out of those wet clothes," said Phillip to my husband, "or they won't let you into the hospital." He led Roger to the house, and as the door closed behind him, I heard Phillip ask, "How did you manage to get here so quickly? Cosette told us your car had broken down."

I didn't hear Roger's reply, because a second contraction had swiftly followed the first. "I think it's time to go," I told my sister.

Our son was born several hours later.

It wasn't until everyone had gone home and Roger, baby Louis, and I were alone that I asked him about *la chasse galerie*. "When I stopped at the tavern to phone you about the car," Roger explained, "I heard several men talking about how lousy the beer was. One fellow suggested flying down to a great pub he knew near the lake. When I heard that they were flying right past our camp, I told them about the baby and asked if I could join them. I thought they were talking about a seaplane. You could have knocked me over with a feather when they pulled out a canoe, pushed me into the front seat, and started paddling it up into the sky, just the way Maman described in her story. I tell you, Cosette, it was the fastest and smoothest flight I have ever taken! Maybe the airlines should invest in a fleet of canoes!"

"I still don't believe what happened, and I saw you with my own eyes," I exclaimed. "Still, it makes me rather uneasy. If the folktales are true, then that canoe was powered by the devil. I don't want my son growing up with a father who owes his soul to Satan. You'd better go to church right away and pray to *le bon Dieu* to save your soul, just in case."

That's just what Roger did.

Nicodemus

SOMERSET COUNTY

It was the fall of 1885 when the farmer's wife came to the barn to complain about a banging noise she heard in the kitchen. The trees were awash with fall color as she leaned through the wide double doors and said: "Would you please make sure the shutters are nailed on good and tight? They've been banging against the house all morning. I keep running to the front door, thinking someone has come to visit."

The farmer frowned. "What wind? The air has been still all morning."

His wife frowned. "That can't be. The shutters are knocking against the house."

The couple stared at one another in puzzlement, then went to investigate. They walked around the house, testing every shutter. None of them moved. The farmer's wife shivered and pulled her shawl tight around herself. "That is very strange."

"Ayup," the farmer agreed. His missus did not make up tales. If she heard the shutters banging, then the shutters had been banging. Without any wind. "Could be a forerunner," he offered after much cogitation. "Let's wait and see what happens next."

NICODEMUS

What happened next was alarming. The family went to bed at dusk, as usual, but were shortly awakened by a tremendous din from below. Banging and crashing and strange metallic twanging shook the entire house. The farmer leapt out of bed, lit the lantern, and ran downstairs, followed by his wife and granddaughter. To his astonishment, he saw chairs hopping across the floor, while the massive dining table tried to shimmy after them. The dishes had removed themselves from storage and were clattering around on the shelves and counters. And the tinware was dancing. There was no other way to describe it. The pieces bounced and twisted around and bowed whenever they encountered another piece of tinware.

"Is the spirit in the kitchen having a frolic?" his granddaughter asked timidly. She watched the madness from a safe perch halfway down the staircase.

"So it would seem," the farmer's wife said, struggling to keep her voice calm. "We should let the spirit get on with it," she added, chivying her granddaughter gently upstairs. "Grampie will take care of it."

The farmer knew an order when he heard one. He hastily grabbed a jug of whiskey as it twirled past and took a slug or two for courage. Then he stepped into the supernatural chaos and recited the Lord's Prayer. Nothing changed. He tried quoting the Twenty-Third Psalm. Still nothing.

They needed to summon the preacher, he decided. He went upstairs to dress, but his missus told him the preacher was away for a few weeks, visiting kin down south. "Maybe if he stayed where he was supposed to, this wouldn't have happened," he grumbled.

At midnight, the racket ceased as abruptly as it started. The farmer went to assess the damage. There were a few dents in the tinware and nicks on the floorboards, but everything else was fine. The furnishings had returned to their rightful place and even the whiskey jug was back where it belonged. He shook his head and went to bed.

By midday, the phantom hijinks were the talk of the town. The farmer's wife complained to the neighbor, who told her sisters, who told all their friends. At twilight, a small crowd gathered in the farmer's yard, agog with excitement. Everyone wanted to see the ghost in action. The farmer told his uninvited guests: "You are welcome to wait outside. I am going to get some shut-eye."

The family went upstairs to bed, trying to ignore the whispers and shuffling coming from the waiting neighbors. They had barely gone to sleep when the whole house shook from top to bottom as the cutlery and tinware and furniture crashed into exuberant life.

The farmer reached the bottom step with his lantern at the same time his uninvited guests burst through his front door. Everyone exclaimed and gaped at the hopping furniture, the musical tinware, and the spinning plates. He motioned them back onto the porch, where they could observe the scene through the windows.

"The spirits are among us," shouted one woman, her eyes as wide as saucers.

"It is the work of the devil," another neighbor cried. The farmer couldn't tell if the man was excited or repulsed by the idea.

"Looks like you got on the wrong side of a witch," said a lumberman who had refused to be ousted. He tried without success to tame one of the hopping chairs.

The celebratory furnishings ceased their dance at midnight, and the crowd slowly dispersed, abuzz with excitement. The farmer and his missus stayed up long afterward, cleaning up the mess the crowd had made while attempting to tame the wild spirit. The farmer was so exhausted he fell into bed with his boots on and slept so soundly he almost missed the morning milking.

"Why did Demus come back?" the farmer's granddaughter asked over breakfast.

"Who is Demus?" the farmer asked.

"The spirit that haunts this house," she replied.

"Is that its name?" his missus asked.

Their granddaughter shrugged. "I don't know. That's what I call him."

The farmer asked her if she could see the spirit. "No," she replied. "But last night I could hear him chuckling. He's not very nice."

A large crowd filled the yard the next evening. There were many faces the farmer did not recognize. People had come from out of town to see the ghostly show. The farmer told his missus: "You and the girl get some rest. I'll manage the visitors." He gave his womenfolk some cork earplugs he had whittled and sent them upstairs to sleep. Then he went outside to talk with the gathered crowd.

The ghostly dance started right on schedule, one hour after dusk. Hoping to maintain control of the situation, the farmer invited small groups to observe the crazy antics of the spirit through the house windows. By midnight, everyone had seen the chaotic dance of the furnishings, tinware, and dishes. Even the most skeptical among their uninvited guests were now believers. Following the established pattern, the ghostly show stopped abruptly at midnight.

Random chaos occurred every evening thereafter, and the crowds continued to grow. People from neighboring towns drove for miles to see the preternatural sight. Then on Sunday, dusk came and went without any sign of the spirit. To the disappointment of the crowd, the house remained still and silent. "The evil spirit must be bound by the holy day," one neighbor opined. "Perhaps it fears excision if it manifests on Sundays."

At ten o'clock, the farmer sent everyone away and locked the front door. Any lingering busybodies could watch through the windows, he decided wearily. He was finally going to get some rest.

"Maybe Demus is gone for good," the farmer's wife said wistfully just before he dozed off.

But the spirit was back to its antics on Monday night, louder than ever. It caused more damage to the house this time, as if it was eager to make up for the lost day. The few hopefuls who had gathered in the farmer's yard on Monday spread the word of the spirit's return, and a larger crowd appeared on Tuesday.

"I hate all this fuss," the farmer's wife complained. "We should charge for entrance. At least then we'd have some compensation for this nightmare. Between the destruction caused by the phantom and the mess made by the crowds, we won't have a farm left by the time the preacher returns from his trip."

The farmer's eyes widened, his Yankee thrift coming to the fore. "We should charge for entrance," he echoed reverently.

His wife looked up sharply and then smiled. "That's the spirit," she said to her husband.

"I thought Demus was the spirit," their granddaughter said, looking up from her schoolbooks.

"There's more than one kind," the missus told her. "Do your schoolwork."

That evening, the farmer charged ten cents for every person who wished to observe the haunting from his yard. To his surprise, everyone was more than willing to pay. As if to show its approval of the scheme, the spirit put on such a good show that its antics could be heard clear across the road. By the time the ghostly phenomenon ceased at midnight, the farmer had a gleam in his eye and a goodly sum in his pocket.

"At this rate, we won't need to fix up the farm. We can buy a new one," he gloated to the missus.

"I like it here," she replied, but didn't press the matter. Having money in the bank would keep them comfortable in their waning years. And there was their granddaughter's future to be thought of.

"I need to buy more tinware," the farmer said distractedly. "I'll just run out to the store."

Word of the haunted house spread throughout the region. People came in droves to see the nightly displays. For the hundreds who came on foot, the farmer charged ten cents a head. Spectators who came in wagons were charged an entire quarter to park on his property, and they happily paid to see the ghost show. Many folks camped overnight on the grounds, watching the supernatural show from the comfort and warmth of their campfires.

The family was well on their way to permanent prosperity. The crazy spirit had gone from bane to blessing in their opinion, and they would have happily let things continue in this supernatural fashion if not for the coming of the mediator.

One afternoon, someone banged thunderously on the front door. Startled, the farmer looked up from the early meal his wife had prepared. He had made it clear that no one was to disturb the family until dusk. Annoyed, he dropped his napkin beside his plate and stalked to the door, just as a deep voice bellowed: "Open up, in the name of the Lord."

The farmer flung the portal wide and found himself face-to-face with the most flamboyant figure he'd ever seen. The tall man wore robes and carried a shepherd's crook. A white cloth around his neck was inscribed with the words: "Mediator of the Nineteenth Century."

"Who the devil are you?" demanded the farmer.

"I am the mediator," the man intoned. "I have been sent by heaven to lay this ghost."

The farmer slammed the door in his face. He did not want a mediator. He did not want the spirit to be laid. He was making money hand-over-fist from the haunting, and he wanted it to go on as long as possible.

The farmer peered out at the crowd gathered in the yard, and saw the flamboyant figure standing among them, shepherd's crook planted firmly in the ground, blazing eyes fixed on the house. His missus came to stand beside him, and her eyes grew wide when she saw the newcomer. "Do you know who that is?" she asked breathlessly.

"He calls himself the mediator," the farmer said grumpily. "Whatever that means."

"That's Mediator Brown," she gasped. "He lives near Elliotsville, and it is said he is the only person in these parts who is empowered to act as a mediator between God and man."

"They were talking about him during recess," their granddaughter piped up suddenly from her seat at the table. "Everyone was telling stories about how Mediator Brown could tame wild animals, cure diseases, bless and curse people, and lay ghosts. Has he come to deal with Demus?"

"I hope not," the farmer muttered.

His wife gave him a reproving nudge. "You must set a good example, dear," she whispered. "Remember we are a Christian family."

By the time the family finished their early dinner, the crowd was in an uproar over the presence of Mediator Brown. They wanted to see what the famous ghost buster could do against such an active spirit. The farmer was overwhelmed with pleas, requests, demands, and direct orders from nearly everyone he knew. Even his neighbors, who had developed a blasé approach to the spirit, were agog with excitement.

Shortly after dark, the house crashed into supernatural life, table and chairs hopping and shuffling, plates and cutlery dancing around, tinware crashing. Reluctantly, the farmer beckoned for the mediator to approach the house. Brown stalked through the door, mumbling in a language he could not understand. It sounded like he was reciting something. Or maybe he was praying?

The crowd pressed as close to the doors and windows as possible so they could watch the mediator. He waved his hands, making mysterious gestures over the dancing furnishings and crashing cutlery. Then he slammed the bottom of his shepherd's crook into the floor and proclaimed in sepulchral tones: "Ghost, begone! I, the mediator, command it."

Instantly, the racket ceased. The tables and chairs stopped hopping, plates and cutlery flew to their proper place, and the tinware went silent. The crowd gasped so loudly no one heard the farmer cursing quietly in the background.

Brown exited the house in triumph to the cheers of the gathering. He accepted their admiration for several minutes before retreating to the orchard where he'd set up a small camp for himself. The most daring members of the crowd followed to inquire about the ghost.

The mediator smiled mysteriously as he set a frying pan over the fire and began cooking his dinner. "It was an evil spirit called Nicodemus," he said. "He came from the fourth hell and had four stripes down his back." Everyone gasped. "No need to worry, my friends," the mediator said soothingly. "All is well now with this house. The spirit is banished and will not return."

Talking excitedly with one another, the crowd slowly dispersed. They had witnessed an extraordinary phenomenon they would remember all their days. Mediator Brown had banished an evil spirit right before their very eyes!

Standing away from the firelight, the farmer felt chills running down his spine. His granddaughter called the spirit "Demus." Was that short for Nicodemus? She said she could hear the dark spirit chuckling when it pulled its tricks in the house. Maybe it *was* time for the spirit to be gone. Although, he mused, if the mediator had left it one or even two more weeks, they could have afforded a bigger house and sent their granddaughter to a fancy finishing school. The thought made the farmer so mad that he stalked over to the mediator, gave him a tongue lashing for spoiling his business, and sent him on his way.

The spirit of Nicodemus was never seen or heard of again.

18

The Other List

PORTLAND

I sat praying in the first pew long after the congregation left the church. The kneeler was hard and my position uncomfortable, but it did not matter. I would stay there forever if it helped, though I was no longer sure it would.

They say God works in mysterious ways, but at the moment I was looking for miraculous, not mysterious. I clutched the Saint Anthony prayer card in my hand, hoping against all hope and trying not to weep.

"Oh holy Saint Anthony, gentlest of saints, your love for God and Charity for his creatures made you worthy, when on earth, to possess miraculous powers," I murmured. Over the last bitter weeks, I had committed the entirety of the unfailing prayer to memory.

A shadow fell over me. The priest was standing in the aisle, debating whether or not to speak. I know what he saw. A young woman in a business casual suit, not a hair out of place. She looked well put together, save for the dark circles around her eyes and a frame that was too thin after weeks of distress and pain. Making up his mind, the father came and knelt beside me.

THE OTHER LIST

"Any word?" he asked. And I began to weep. He waited patiently, handing me a handkerchief and offering a consoling pat on my shoulder.

"They want to turn off life support," I said at last. "Two of the doctors think she is brain dead, and the third is losing hope. My brother is being pressured by the hospital, by insurance, by everyone. We keep praying to Saint Anthony for a miracle, but nothing is happening. It's hard to have faith when no one seems to be listening."

It seemed like a simple accident. During a pickup softball game, a line-drive hit my sister-in-law in the head, blackening her right eye. The doctor who examined her found no concussion or any other injury. But two nights later, Faith had a terrible seizure and Frank called 9-1-1. She was rushed to the hospital and immediately into surgery because she was bleeding heavily inside her brain cavity. The entire extended family rushed to the hospital in various stages of undress to support Frank and Faith.

We were all present when the physician told my brother that Faith might not make it, and if she did, she probably would not be the same person. The damage to her brain was thought to be extensive. No one was willing to accept this prognosis. We started a prayer vigil, handing out Saint Anthony cards to everyone in the family and all our friends. Families brought food to the house so Frank wouldn't have to cook, and Father Morris held a special prayer mass for everyone. And then we waited. And waited. And waited some more for Faith to wake up.

Frank slept every night on the floor of the hospital room. He refused to leave. They'd only been married for a year and were preparing to start their family. He would not let go of his wife and the life they had built together. We took turns urging him to eat and shower and get some exercise. He was almost as thin and frail as Faith underneath her tubes and IVs and everything else keeping her alive.

"Frank doesn't know what to do," I said finally, wiping away my tears. "He doesn't want to pull the plug on his wife. He asked me what Jesus would do in these circumstances, and I didn't know what to say."

I took a deep shuddering breath and shook my head. "You know what's the worst thing for me? I keep dreaming of the family here in church on All Souls Day. We are listening to you read the list of those who have died in the past year, and you call out F . . . Faith's name. And in that moment, I realize we've lost her." I broke down again.

"But Faith isn't dead," Father Morris said gently. "And Saint Anthony still performs miracles."

I looked at him out of my raccoon eyes and whispered: "But will he have one for us?"

We were silent for a time. Then the father said: "All Souls Day is next weekend."

I nodded.

"When do the doctors need an answer about life support?" he asked. I could tell he was thinking hard about something.

"Soon," I choked on the word. "There's still one hold-out, Faith's primary care physician. But once they are all in agreement . . ." I couldn't finish.

"If you knew for certain that she was brain-dead, would that help Frank make the decision?" the father asked.

My eyes widened: "It would. If he knew her soul was already gone to Jesus, then he wouldn't feel so . . . guilty . . . pulling the plug. But how can anyone know for sure?"

The father looked uncomfortable. "You mentioned the list of the newly deceased that we read on All Souls Day," he said slowly. "Not many know about it, but there is . . . another list."

"Another list?" I asked blankly. I stared at the altar and the flickering candles, as if they held the answer to this new mystery.

"At midnight on All Saints Day, a . . . Being of some kind . . . calls out the names of the congregants who will die in the upcoming year," the father said.

I straightened in shock. "That's just a Halloween folktale," I cried, indignant that my priest would pull such a prank on a grieving congregant. "They say the devil calls out the names of those who are going to hell in the upcoming year."

"It is not a folktale," he said. "It's a fact. The Being who calls the names is not the devil. I am not sure who it is. Some believe it is the Angel of Death. Very few have heard of the ceremony and fewer still attend it."

I glared at him. "Then how do you know about it?"

"I have witnessed it myself," the father said softly. "One All Hallows Eve, I fell asleep in this very pew after hours of prayer and meditation. I was awakened by a Voice calling out the name of the parishioner for whom I had been praying. The Voice seemed to vibrate in my bones. The parishioner's name was but the first on a long list spoken by the unseen figure on the stroke of midnight. At first, I thought it was a dream. But by the end of twelve months, every person on that list had passed away. That's when I knew I'd stumbled onto a sacred mystery."

I was shaken by his story. He spoke with such conviction that I believed him. The father had never lied to me.

"Then why tell me?" I asked.

"Because you have need," he said. "I have attended the All Hallows Eve ceremony every year since that long ago day, and it has helped me prepare my congregation for the trials that lay before them. If Faith's name is on the list this year, then you will know that she has been called home. I'd like you to join me here, on All Hallows Eve, to bear witness to this year's list."

I drew a shaky breath, then agreed. It seemed ludicrous, but we were desperate. We needed an answer; Frank needed an answer. Maybe this was it.

I didn't know what one wore to a Sacred List Ceremony, but since it was a record of those who were about to die, I figured all black was safe. When I met the priest on the porch of the church at 11:30 p.m. on October 31, I was pleased to see he also wore black vestments, with a purple stole and a funeral pall. According to folklore, the porch was the traditional place for such a vigil, but the father welcomed me inside the sanctuary and gestured for me to sit in the last pew, while he stood vigil at the back of the church.

The only light came from the candles burning in the votive stands. The air was cool and still, and the silence was so thick I could hear my own breath. I held my Saint Anthony card in my hand and prayed that this moment would contain the answer we needed.

The only person who knew about tonight's vigil was Frank. My brother had broken down over our shared lunch on Friday. The family physician said he needed to make a decision. I begged Frank to wait one more day and told him the story the priest had shared with me.

"If the . . . the Being calls her name, we will know it is time," I said. "I'll phone you directly after the ceremony. Please keep your cell on."

It says a lot about his state of mind that my skeptical brother accepted both the story and my part in it as gospel truth. "I'll be waiting," he said.

I was deep in my meditations when the deep toll of a bell rang through the sanctuary. It jerked me out of my trance, and I opened my eyes. A glowing white light hovered above the altar, forming slowly into a shape—neither woman nor man nor beast. It was nothing my earthly mind could register properly, but its holiness was palpable. This was no devil. It was a . . . Being. Maybe an archangel? I had no words to describe it.

The bell tolled again, and the Being spoke a woman's name. It was one of the elderly in our parish who was ill with pneumonia. The funeral bell tolled again. When the echoes died, the Being spoke the next name. It was a teenager who attended the local high school. The funeral bell tolled.

Name after name rolled forth from the Being at the altar. The elderly. The sick. The young. The healthy. They were all represented in the List. It might only have been my imagination, but I started seeing wispy white figures make their way down the center aisle, past the father guarding the doorway, and out toward the cemetery. The sight raised the hairs on the back of my neck.

I listened intently for Faith's name. I expected to feel anxiety and anguish, but the deep calm of the sanctuary and the presence of the holy Being filled me with peace. No matter what happened this evening, Faith was safe in God's hands. There was nothing to fear.

The bell tolled three times in a row. The father bowed to the Being hovering over the altar, and I bowed my head too. Abruptly, the bright light vanished, leaving us alone in the sanctuary. It took a moment for my eyes to adjust to the dim glow of the votive candles. And another for me to register what I had heard. Or rather, what I *hadn't* heard.

Eyes widening, I turned to look at the father for confirmation. "She wasn't on the list," I gasped. "Faith's name wasn't on the list!"

The father nodded. "It was not on the list," he said. "I'm expecting a miracle."

And that's when my phone started buzzing frantically in my pocket. I'd turned it off for the ceremony, but it had turned itself back on and the vibration echoed through the church.

I grabbed it out of my purse and put it on speaker. The caller was my brother Frank.

"He was here," Frank shouted through the speaker. "I woke up just now and Saint Anthony was here! He was standing by the bed, holding Faith's hand. He looked just like the picture on the prayer cards. He smiled at me and said: 'Do you believe in miracles?' And then all the lights and alarms on the machines went crazy, and Faith opened her eyes!"

"Dear God," I breathed.

Frank took a shuddering breath and continued: "The night nurses came running into the room and skidded to a halt when they saw Saint Anthony. He smiled at them and then he vanished into thin air. The nurses were too shocked to speak. Then the alarm recalled them to their duties, and they thrust me out into the hallway so they could work on Faith. That's when I called you."

"I knew it!" I shouted excitedly when he finished. "I knew a miracle was coming because Faith's name wasn't on the list!"

"It wasn't on the list?" Frank repeated.

"No! She's going to live," I said, tears streaming down my face as the truth settled into my heart.

The father's eyes were wet as he gestured for the phone. I handed it to him so he could speak with Frank, and then I opened the kneeler and knelt with my forehead on the back of the next pew, weeping tears of joy. Saint Anthony had come on All Saints Day and given us a miracle. And I'd seen something miraculous. Something . . . some One that very few people ever encountered directly. I wondered what it meant for my future. I shrugged away the thought. For now, it was time to rejoice with the one who was rejoicing. And perhaps later this year, I could assist the father as he ministered with those who mourned.

19

Dance with the Devil

LUBEC

Janet softly opened the door to the kitchen and peeked inside. No one was present. Sighing with relief, she crept silently into the house, closing the door whisper-soft before jogging lightly upstairs with her carefully wrapped bundle.

Her parents were adamantly opposed to dancing. Their religion banned it and her father often declaimed against the sinners who frequented the local dancehall. "They've sold their souls," he shouted after reading about a successful ball in the local newspaper. "The devil will show up at the dancehall one day and claim every person there!"

Janet thought this was nonsense. It was the 1920s, not the Dark Ages. No modern person believed in the devil anymore. She shook her head over such out-of-date notions. Still, while she was living in her parents' home, she tried to follow their rules. Or at the very least, to keep them in the dark when she planned to attend the weekly dance with her friends. If they learned of her intention, they would lock her in her room!

Janet removed the sparkling red dress from the bag and hung it in the closet to air. Then she snuck downstairs to find the iron and board so she could press it. She looked magnificent

DANCE WITH THE DEVIL

in the dress, or so the salesperson said. The fellows at the dance tonight would vie for her attention. It was going to be the best evening of her life.

She heard her parents come in while she was doing her hair. Her mother called up the stairs: "Dinner will be ready in a few minutes, Janet."

She called back: "I'm not hungry, Mama. I've got a headache, so I'm going to bed early."

Janet heard her mother's footsteps approaching, so she swiftly closed the closet door, jumped into bed, and turned off the light. Her mother came into the room and laid a hand on her forehead. "Can I get you some aspirin, Jenny-girl?" she asked. "Or a cup of tea?"

"I've taken some aspirin already," Janet replied, making her voice sound drowsy. "I think I just need some sleep."

"All right," her mother said, dropping a kiss on her forehead. "I'll let you rest."

Janet waited impatiently until her mother went downstairs and told her father their little girl would be "just fine in the morning." Then she leapt out of bed, turned on the light, and finished doing her hair.

Her parents were eating dinner in the kitchen, when she crept down the back staircase in her sparkling red dress, her dance slippers in hand. Once she was out in the yard, she put her heels on, drew her shawl around her shoulders, and hurried down the block to meet her friends.

As soon as their group walked into the dancehall, all the men turned to look at Janet. She was luminous in her sparkling red dress, her face lively and bright with excitement. The men crowded around, fighting with each other to dance with her.

Her friends exchanged startled glances and faded into the background. Everyone else at the dance watched her with envy. Janet didn't care—she was popular at last, and she was going to make the most of it.

Janet was standing near the back drinking punch with her latest dance partner when the music stopped abruptly. Craning her head, she saw a stunningly handsome man wearing a black suit and red vest entering the room. Women gravitated toward him from every part of the dancehall, fluttering and simpering in a manner oddly reminiscent of the men's behavior when Janet first arrived at the dance.

The music restarted, and the man in the red vest swept a lovely blonde out onto the dance floor, and the other ladies sighed with regret. Janet's partner claimed her hand, and they joined the others. It was a change dance, and every few steps Janet had a new partner. She kept an eye on the devilishly handsome man in the red vest as he drew closer down the line. Each woman he danced with sparkled radiantly in his presence and then drooped when he moved along. To her disappointment, the song ended before the man in the red vest reached her. Too bad.

When the band took a short break, everyone flocked to the refreshment tables. Janet was plied with food and drink by several eager suitors, and she lost track of the man in the red vest. She did notice something strange about several females standing nearby. Each of them had a glowing patch on their left shoulder or waist. It looked like a clawed handprint. Several men also bore the mark, though it appeared on their right sleeve where a person might have clasped them while shaking hands. How strange. Were these people in some kind of secret club?

At that moment, the band returned, and Janet was swept out on the dance floor. Everyone was busy laughing and flirting and changing partners. The man in the red vest was in high demand. Women kept cutting in to dance with him, and several catfights broke out. He just laughed and stepped aside to dance with the next woman in line.

During the next refreshment break, the man in the red vest approached Janet. "Dance with me," he commanded with a devilish smile that made her weak in the knees. Janet stammered her assent, completely stunned by this gorgeous man. He led her out on the dance floor, and music sprang up at once as if on command. Janet found herself performing better than she ever had before, easily following the man in the red vest through elaborate moves she had never learned. Everyone stopped dancing to watch them, and Janet felt elated. They were the center of attention.

Then the man in the red vest spun Janet around. At first, she was invigorated by the fancy display, but he kept repeating the movement until she gasped for air. Frightened, she tried to step out of the spin, but her partner twirled her so rapidly she could not escape his grasp. Janet's feet were burning, and the floor seemed to melt beneath her as she gazed in horror at her partner's face. That's when she realized that his eyes glowed like red flames and two horns protruded from his forehead. The man's smile was pure evil as he twirled her too fast to draw breath. "The devil will show up at the dancehall one day," he murmured mockingly in her ear.

The dancehall darkened dramatically, and a sulfurous-smelling mist swirled in from the doors and ceiling, hiding Janet and her partner from the crowd. The watchers gasped and murmured admiringly over the special effects. When the mist cleared, the man in the red vest bowed mockingly to the assembly, and they burst into applause. Then he gestured toward a woman standing at the front of the crowd. In the dim light, a clawed handprint glowed brightly on her shoulder. Everyone gasped, and looked down at their own garments, most of which were claw-marked. When the dancers glanced back at the man in the red vest, they saw his true form: horned head, clawed hands, cloven hooves, and leathery tail.

The devil smiled wickedly at the assembly and said: "Thank you for welcoming me to your dance. I will see many of you again soon." The clawed handprints with which he had marked each dancer pulsed a vivid red color as he spoke. He bowed mockingly and disappeared behind a curtain of fire. The smell of brimstone and sulfur swept across the room as the panicked crowd ran for the doors.

No one noticed until the next morning that Janet was missing. She was the last woman to dance with the devil that fateful night, and she was never seen again.

The Wizard

HALLOWELL

When you saw old Uncle Kaler puttering around among the roses in the garden at the back of his house, you would never have taken him for the local wizard. No sir. Uncle Kaler was small and wrinkled and bald. He lived all alone on Loudon Hill and he was always giving flowers to folk passing on their way to Cobbossee or the Hook. 'Course, many of the folk traveling that road were not really passing at all. Oh, they all had some trumped-up excuse for their journey, but they were really coming to see Uncle Kaler, wanting good luck charms, or love potions, or cattle cures.

But potions and amulets were just his sideline business; Uncle Kaler was best known for his ability to manipulate the weather. He could whistle up a whirlwind, start and stop a storm, make it snow in summer, or send a warm blast of air to heat the coldest day. People consulting Uncle Kaler for the first time were sometimes amused by the antics of the wrinkled, elfin man as he tested the wind with his finger or twirled his soup spoon around in the air. But when they got home, they would find their pond suddenly filled to the brim due to a cloudburst,

THE WIZARD

or the ruined orchard at the back of their property cleared by a freak tornado, and they never laughed at Uncle Kaler again.

'Course, manipulating the weather is a tricky business, and sometimes it can get away from a body, even one as talented as Uncle Kaler. The incident I remember best came on a warm and misty summer evening a few years back. Uncle Kaler had spent the evening working among his roses, and as dusk fell he gathered an armload of yellow blossoms and brought them into the kitchen. As he was fetching out a vase for his treasures, he heard a horse speeding up the hill and stopping right outside his door.

Uncle Kaler opened the door. A youngish fellow appeared panting on his doorstep, holding a pretty young lady by the hand. Uncle Kaler recognized the young man at once, though he did not know the young lady. William had spent much of his time sailing the seas, and had done quite well for himself. His parents were very proud of their youngest boy, though some looked down upon him because his family came from poor farming stock.

"Are you Mr. Kaler?" William asked breathlessly.

"Yes, indeed," said Uncle Kaler heartily. "And I am at your service."

"Mr. Kaler, Elizabeth and I are on our way to Hallowell to be married. But her relatives don't approve of the match. Somehow they found out we were eloping tonight. You can hear them behind us!"

And indeed, Uncle Kaler could hear the sound of bloodhounds baying away down the river.

"Mr. Kaler, if you don't help us, they will murder us both. Please, sir. I've been saving up. I can offer you a hundred

Spanish millers for the worst weather you've got, and I will give you another hundred when we come back."

Without a word, Uncle Kaler disappeared into the house. He went to his old sea chest standing under the window and took out a leather bag. Going back to the door, he handed the bag to William and said: "Go back down the road and release the contents of this bag. Then throw the bag into the millstream. When you return, you will be able to continue your journey undisturbed."

William looked at the bag suspiciously, but did as he was told.

While Elizabeth gazed anxiously down the road after her bridegroom, Uncle Kaler went back into the kitchen to get some roses. Handing them to Elizabeth, he smiled shyly and said: "A wedding present from your good friend Uncle Kaler."

Elizabeth blushed happily and thanked him.

A moment later, William rode back up the road. "I've done it," he said. "But nothing happened. If you've played us false, Mr. Kaler . . ."

He tried to look threatening but only managed to look frightened. Uncle Kaler just smiled.

"Listen," he said.

There came a low grumble of thunder from the southwest. It increased in volume, and the wind rose sharply and began to pummel the tops of the trees.

"Is it a cyclone?" Elizabeth squeaked in terror.

"Just a cloudburst," Uncle Kaler said soothingly. "In about five minutes not one of those hounds will be able to find you. No, no, keep your money," he added as William tried to press the Spanish millers on him. "Buy a pretty house for your new wife."

Elizabeth blushed at the word *wife* and then boldly kissed Uncle Kaler's cheek. They mounted the horse, and Uncle Kaler called: "Good luck to you, from a man who can make his own luck."

They rode quickly toward Hallowell through the gathering storm. The thunder was roaring almost continuously now, and lightning lit up the sky as a torrent of rain suddenly drenched Uncle Kaler where he stood by the garden gate.

"Hmm," he said, waving his hand. The rain parted and fell on either side of him. "I think I may have made that bag a tad bit too strong. Well, at least it will give those young folk a chance. It would never do for them to get caught."

He shook himself and was instantly dry. Then he walked up the path to the door, the rain falling away before it reached him and then pouring back into the gap when he had passed.

"Perhaps one teaspoon less of tansy," he muttered, closing his door against the raging torrent. Uncle Kaler opened the door again and told the rain: "You stay away from my roses!" The rain around the house stopped instantly. Nodding his approval, he shut the door and went to bed. All around Hallowell and the surrounding towns, a great storm raged all night long, except over Uncle Kaler's garden.

The next morning dawned bright and clear. Uncle Kaler whistled cheerfully as he went out into his garden. But a strange sound met his ears. Above the chirping of the birds came the rushing sound of water running through a gorge. The millstream had never sounded like that before, even when it flooded. Going to investigate, Uncle Kaler found that the millstream had been replaced by a raging torrent coursing through a deep gorge.

It was filled with uprooted trees and brush. The mill itself was completely gone.

Following this new landscape, Uncle Kaler soon spotted the huge boulder that was once part of the foundation of the mill. It had been swept clean into the river and would create a nasty obstacle in the future to anyone traveling upon it. A long muddy point stretched out into the river from the mouth of the brook. The grindstone from the mill was nowhere to be seen.

"Definitely too much tansy," said Uncle Kaler. Then he shrugged and went home to his roses.

21

The Cursed Tomb

BUCKSPORT

Bucksport may seem like a sleepy little town to folks just passing through. But let me tell you, we have a local legend that has kept people talking for more than a hundred years. The tale goes something like this.

There was a beautiful widow woman who lived just outside of a small town here in New England. Folks would go to her for herbal remedies whenever they were ill, but some claimed there was a dark side to her. She had a young son who was deformed from birth, and many people in that Puritanical town reckoned that was a sign from God that she had sold her soul to the devil.

There came a hot summer with little rain. The crops dried up, the trees lost their leaves, and many farm animals took ill. Then the preacher's wife noticed that the widow was still doing a brisk business outside of town. Her garden was thriving despite the drought.

"It's the work of the devil, sure," she told her neighbors.

Others noticed the woman's industry and relative prosperity in this time of drought, and they were jealous of her success. In the manner of this wicked old world, they began looking

THE CURSED TOMB

for flaws, and when they found none—she was virtuous, kind, helpful, hardworking—they invented them.

One Sunday after services, a crowd gathered in the churchyard to discuss the matter.

"The widow walked past my house, and my cow died the next evening," one farmer complained.

"I saw a figure flying over my barn last night, and this morning a horse kicked my husband in the stomach," the blacksmith's wife reported.

"A black cat crossed my path on the way to the mercantile, and when it looked up at me, it had the herb-woman's eyes," a kettle tinker said. "I turned my wagon around and went the other way, so she wouldn't ruin my business."

When the widow's neighbor came seeking a love potion for her daughter to use on a wealthy suitor, the goodwife refused her request. The two women spoke strong words against one another in front of several witnesses, and it was considered another black mark against the widow. Not long after, the neighbor died unexpectedly, and the whole town pointed an accusing finger at the widow, even though the examining physician said it was heart failure. The widow was dragged in front of the local justice to stand trial for witchcraft and sorcery.

Justice Jonathan Buck was a stern man with a strict moral code. His word was law in that town, and evil of any kind would not be tolerated. When the citizens brought a charge of witchcraft against the widow, he immediately threw her in jail. Justice Buck considered witchcraft an act of blasphemy against the Creator. The widow's fate was sealed the moment she was accused of the crime. Her trial was a sham, filled with speculation rather than fact, and its result was predetermined.

The widow was condemned to death for the use of sorcery against her neighbors.

The widow was taken to the center of town and burnt at the stake for her crimes. As the flames licked around her long skirts, the condemned woman cried: "Jonathan Buck, listen to these words, the last my tongue shall utter. Today, I am crushed beneath the foot of your injustice, but it will not always be so." The widow's face creased with agony as fire seared her flesh. Drawing a pained breath, she continued: "You will die soon, and thereafter you will be forever beneath me. Over your grave they will erect a stone, and upon that stone the imprint of my foot will appear. Long after your generations have perished from the face of the earth, people from far and near will see my sign upon your tombstone and know that you murdered an innocent woman."

The widow's deformed son was among the crowd, forced by his pious caretakers to watch his mother burned for witchcraft. As the flames devoured the widow, one charred leg fell from the pyre and rolled into the open. Breaking away from his caretakers, the boy ran forward to pick up the limb, the only piece left of his mother. With an oath against Justice Buck, the boy fled into the wilderness, never to return.

Though he showed no sign of remorse during the execution, Jonathan Buck was disturbed by the widow's curse. He became a fitful sleeper, plagued by terrible dreams. His business dealings also took a turn for the worse. His bid to build a shipyard was denied and he was offered a mediocre deal in its place. He chose instead to sail up the Penobscot River with a survey team in 1762 to review several potential plantation sites. Two years later, Jonathan Buck brought his family to the site designated Plantation No. 1 to establish a new settlement in Maine.

A strong leader, Jonathan Buck built the first store, the first sawmill, the first gristmill, and the first boat. The new community was thriving when America went to war with the British, but matters took a turn for the worse after the Patriots were defeated during the Penobscot Expedition. Jonathan Buck, now a colonel in the Continental Army, had a scant few hours to move his wife and daughter to safety before the British burned Plantation No. 1 to the ground. His settlement in ruins, Colonel Buck was forced to walk more than two hundred miles south to Massachusetts, where he resumed his place in the Continental Army and took up residence with his grown sons.

Following the peace treaty of 1783, Colonel Buck returned to the Penobscot River and rebuilt the settlement at Plantation No. 1. Known among the colonists as an industrious and honorable man, Colonel Buck died in 1795, and the settlers named the town Bucksport in his honor.

The widow's curse had long been forgotten when the colonel's descendants erected a grand monument in his honor. Then a strange discoloration appeared upon the tomb, growing more apparent each week. The outline of a woman's leg and foot was clearly displayed in the granite. The family tried to have the mark removed, but each time it was sanded away, the image returned. Rumors spread rapidly about the source and meaning of the mark, and soon the story was reported in newspapers across the country.

Today, the legend of the cursed tombstone has many versions. Details have changed as the story was retold from coast to coast. However, one fact endures: Colonel Buck's monument—built in 1852—still bears the image of a woman's leg and foot upon it. You can see it for yourself the next time you are in Bucksport, if you dare.

22

The Sandman

YORK HARBOR

Now, mind you, I cannot prove that Trickey was the meanest, the orneriest, and the roughest fisherman who ever lived and worked in Maine. But if it wasn't him, well, then he came pretty darned close.

Trickey lived at the mouth of the York River. No one associated with him if they could help it, for he was malevolent, wicked, and prickly to boot. He had to keep his fish prices at rock bottom just to get anyone to buy from him. Not, as the wags of York said, that fishing was how he really made a living.

No one in York would have been surprised if they had known, when he died, that Old Trickey was turned over to the devil himself on account of all his misdeeds.

"Well now, Trickey," said the devil, "it seems like you've managed to wound and offend jest about everybody living in and around York. Tut, tut, we have been naughty."

"Not me fault," Trickey grumbled. "They jest dint understand me." A typical complaint that the people of York could all parrot, and the wags at the tavern often did.

"Well, Trickey, this here record says it was your fault," said the devil. "I think you're going to have to hang around this

THE SANDMAN

harbor for a long time, Trickey. Seems like I need someone to bind sand, Trickey. Bind it and haul it 'round this harbor. The sand's looking a bit thin over there. It's going to take a lot of sand, Trickey, before this record's paid!"

"Not me fault," Trickey whined. "Not me fault. They jest dint understand me."

"Oh, I think they understood you just fine," said the devil. "Off you go, then."

And the devil set Trickey to binding and hauling sand with a rope. Old Trickey cursed, and fumed, and fretted, but he was tied to the harbor, and he had to bind the sand with a rope and haul it hither and thither at the devil's bidding.

Now the devil, he liked to play games with Old Trickey. Sometimes, when Trickey got a load of sand set just so, the devil would send a wind in and blow the sand away, just so Trickey would be forced to bind it up again. This enraged Trickey, and he would fume and curse so loud the people 'round the harbor would shake their heads to hear him.

But when a storm began to gather, then the harbor folk would hear Old Trickey at his worst. As the wind and the rain blew ashore, whipping up the waves, the wraith of Old Trickey would fly shrieking over the land. "More rope, more rope," he cried. "More sand, more sand." Old Trickey would bind sand in a fury and then, hauling it to the shore, dump it atop the dunes, then scrape it out and throw it back into the waves.

After many years had passed, Old Trickey got fed up with the devil's tricks. He gathered many lengths of rope and bound sand until he had a veritable mountain. Then he waited for a giant gale to strike shore. When he saw the storm coming,

Old Trickey let out such a shriek of rage that the people of the harbor prayed to the Good Lord to spare them.

Then, as dusk fell and the storm gathered in strength, Old Trickey came roaring inland. The bravest of the harbor folk watched Old Trickey growing larger and larger as he came, hauling his mountain of sand behind him. But even the bravest hid their eyes as Old Trickey blew across the cottages and cabins, strewing sand everywhere as he howled his challenge to the devil. The sand dunes shifted, the storm raged, and Old Trickey met the devil in midair and wrestled with him over the harbor where he had labored so long.

Old Trickey's howling and shrieking continued all night long as he grappled with the devil at the height of the storm. Meanwhile, the fierce wind and rain were whipping the mountain of sand hither and thither, pelting the homes of the harbor folk, shifting old sand dunes, and creating new ones. But toward dawn all went silent. When the harbor folk ventured out of doors the next morning, the landscape was completely new. The sands had shifted and many a garden was now buried under Old Trickey's load. The atmosphere above the harbor was tremulous, and folk knew that Old Trickey was still wrestling with the devil.

But a new breeze sprang up as they watched. It blew away the clouds and heartened the harbor folk so much that they began clearing away all the storm debris and Old Trickey's sand. As they worked, they heard a sudden boom from the surf. The devil had thrown Old Trickey down into the harbor. On the breeze, the breaking waves seemed to mutter: Not me fault. They jest dint understand me.

So Old Trickey went back to his work, grumbling and complaining and cursing his fate. But binding and hauling sand was his doom and everyone, even Old Trickey, knew the devil would never be satisfied with his labor.

Sometimes, though, Old Trickey still gets fed up with the devil's tricks. When he does, Old Trickey the Sandman rises up during the next mighty gale and wrestles with the devil till morning.

23

The Sailor's Dream

KENNEBUNKPORT

The deck swayed ominously beneath my feet. The smell of salt stung my nose, while frozen droplets and the occasional snowflake stung my cheeks. I gazed off the stern of the Isadore, *watching the slowly retreating coastline, and saw seven wooden boxes on the shore. No, not boxes. Funeral caskets. "What in God's name are those for?" I gasped aloud. I wasn't expecting a reply, but an eerie voice answered me out of the rising wind: "They are for the crew of the* Isadore *. . ."*

I woke, trembling from head to toe and covered in a cold sweat. What an awful dream. I had signed articles for the *Isadore*, and I was due onboard in four days. It should be easy, just a short coastal run down to New Orleans and back. Why was I so frightened by the prospect? My wife, bless her heart, got up and poured me a glass of water from the pitcher. I could hardly drink it, my hands trembled so. She rubbed my back until I calmed, then blew out the lantern and told me to sleep. It took a long while for me to obey her.

I discussed the dream with some friends the next morning. "Do you think it's a forerunner?" one sailor asked. A forerunner was a bad omen.

THE SAILOR'S DREAM

"I don't know," I replied honestly. "I may just be nervous to sail under Captain Foss. He's launching the *Isadore* on a Friday. That's bad luck."

I earned my living as a ship's carpenter, and I was proud of the many leagues I'd traveled on the seas. The barque *Isadore* was a new build out of Kennebunkport, and I had signed articles and taken an advance on a month's wages to sail on her maiden voyage to New Orleans with a shipment of hay and potatoes. But I wasn't too sure about the ship's captain. Foss was rated as one of the best skippers in Maine, but he already had a mutiny and a shipwreck to his name.

The way I heard it, four members of Foss's crew mutinied during the maiden voyage of the *Horace*, but the captain subdued the rebellion and confined the miscreants while the ship returned to port. Foss delivered the mutineers to the authorities in Kennebunk, then left the *Horace* anchored outside the Kennebunk River for the next four days while he supervised cargo operations and resupplied the ship. Foss was still ashore one night, sleeping safely in his cozy bed, when a gale blew in and severed the *Horace* from both cables, casting her adrift. The ship struck the ledges off Oakes Neck, lost her rudder *and* her false keel, and finally grounded herself on Boothby's Beach about 150 yards below high-water mark. She was found upright with her masts still standing the next morning, but she'd taken so much damage the insurance companies declared her a total loss. At least the crew got out alive.

There were so many things wrong with that story I did not have enough fingers and toes to count them. Still, there's an old saying: once bitten twice shy. Maybe Captain Foss had learned his lesson and this new journey would go smoothly.

I had errands that took me to the shipyard that morning, and I was surprised by the gloomy silence within. The closer the *Isadore* came to her first voyage, the more morose the shipbuilders became. She was a stout barque of 396 tons burden, and the very best timber was used in her construction. The shipyard should have been filled with last-minute construction and cheerful builders. The silence was disturbing.

More than one carpenter commented on my wan appearance. At first, I shrugged them off, but finally confided my worries to an old seaman I'd known my whole life. By the time I finished, his cheeks were as pale as mine.

"Forerunner," he muttered. "Do you think it's an omen?"

"Maybe I just ate a fish that disagreed with me," I said, using humor to diffuse the conversation. Sailors were a superstitious lot. It didn't take much to spook a crew. I didn't want to give the *Isadore* a bad reputation before her hull touched the sea.

My friend nodded, acknowledging my point. But I could see he did not agree. Considering the rumors swirling around the *Isadore*, he could be right. Materials from the wrecked *Horace* were used to rig the new barque. That did not seem propitious. And on launch day, the *Isadore* stopped suddenly about halfway down the stocks. The crew had quite a time of it getting the barque down to the river. As she plunged into the water, the *Isadore* staggered and reeled so badly the watchers feared that she would go on her beam end. The crew finally stabilized the barque and got her moored to a wharf in the Kennebunk River, but this troublesome beginning was considered an ill omen for the seamen who had signed articles aboard her.

I was not eager to go to bed that night, in spite of my weariness. I stayed next to the warm fire, whittling away at a moose I was carving for my wife, who loved the creatures. Moose were already funny looking, with their bulbous antlers and bell. I enhanced the comic look by adding a sly grin. A moment later, the master and commander of our home snatched the critter from my hand, put it on the mantel, and ordered me to bed. "Aye captain," I saluted smartly. I heard her chuckling over the moose's cheeky smile on my way upstairs.

The deck swayed ominously beneath my feet. The smell of salt stung my nose as I stared at seven wooden caskets on the shore. "They are for the crew of the Isadore *. . ." an eerie voice wailed in my ear.*

I woke with a shout and sat straight up in bed. This was the second time I'd had the same dream. Was it an omen? My wife wrapped me in the spare blanket and snuggled beside me until my shaking ebbed. "I don't like this dream," I murmured in her ear. "Nor do I," she replied solemnly.

I heard whispers everywhere I went the next morning. Word had gotten around about my dream. I knew it would. Sailors gossip. Always have, always would. The dark rings under my eyes just added more fuel to the rumors.

Mine was not the only forerunner dissected by the tavern drinkers that afternoon. I heard about dogs barking at unseen presences, disturbing dreams, and other bad omens. I wasn't the only seaman nervous about serving under Captain Foss. He came from an illustrious line of sailors, but he could be as stubborn as a mule. He didn't believe in fate and wouldn't listen to reason even when it came from other shipmasters.

There were two more days before we set sail: first to Boston and then south to New Orleans. The weather was fair for November, mild and sunny. Even the infamous Maine fog stayed away. These should have been good portents, but all I could think of were seven caskets and a phantom voice on the wind. This made it hard to fall asleep.

The deck swayed ominously beneath my feet, and frozen droplets coated my cheeks. I gazed off the stern of the Isadore *at seven funeral caskets on the cold shore. "What in God's name are those for?" I cried. The voice replied: "They are for the* Isadore . . .*"*

I woke with a mighty roar, rejecting the voice, rejecting the dream. I fell out of bed and landed with a thump in a tangle of blankets, leaving my wife alone on the bare mattress. I'd had the same dream three times in a row. That wasn't an omen. It was a prophecy.

"You'd best speak with the captain," my wife said from atop the bed, her voice very dry.

"Ayup, I'd best do that," I croaked, my mouth dry with fear. I climbed to my feet, picked up the blankets, and got back into bed. I would have to return the advance on my wages, but that was a small price to pay for my life.

Captain Foss was not pleased with me or the returned wages. "Belay that! Where would I find another carpenter at this late hour, pray? You signed the articles; you will sail with the ship. We leave Friday on the tide. Be aboard with the rest of the crew."

"Aye, captain," I said, pocketing the money.

I walked slowly home, shoulders hunched, steps dragging. I barely acknowledged the greetings friends and acquaintances tossed my way, so heavy was the weight upon my mind. "He said no," I told my wife, sinking sadly into the fireside chair. She rubbed his lips thoughtfully, then sat down in her knitting chair opposite mine. "The Good Lord gave you a dream. A prophecy," she said earnestly. "Who is more important to obey? Your earthly captain, or your heavenly one?"

I stared for a long time at the fire, not sure how to answer.

"Get a drink, talk to your friends," my wife said finally. "Have a good think. I will support you no matter what you decide."

My lovely bride—the best wife a man could ever have—shooed me out the front door and shut it in my face. Chuckling despite my fears, I went to my favorite tavern to ruminate over some rum.

One of my good friends sat down on the barstool beside mine. He was second mate for the *Isadore*, and I was sure he knew about my dreams and the failed interview with the captain, but he didn't comment on any of it, which I appreciated. We finished our first round and ordered a second, chatting easily about the upcoming voyage.

"Captain's been in bit of a rage for several days," my friend said abruptly when our second round of drinks arrived. "He keeps hearing about bad omens and portents. Folks believe our New Orleans voyage is doomed. Captain swore at me yesterday. He said if he lost another ship, he hoped his head would be found under the mast."

We winced simultaneously. No one—master, mate, or seaman—should say such a thing, particularly when they planned a Friday launch. Yet another ill omen.

"What would you do, if you were given a prophetic dream?" I asked softly.

The silence went on so long I wasn't sure he heard. Then the second mate took one last swallow of his rum, set his glass down next to mine, and said: "If it were me, I wouldn't go." We nodded solemnly to one another, and he left the tavern without looking back.

By dawn the next morning, I was hidden in an obscure overlook watching the port from afar without being seen. The town was strangely quiet, considering it was the departure day for a brand-new ship. There were more grim faces than happy ones. And the sky was red that morning. Sailor, take warning.

When my absence was noted, a hue and cry went up through port and town. That was my cue. With a farewell glance at the mouth of the Kennebec River, where a crowd would gather this afternoon to see the new ship underway, I shouldered my seaman's kit and walked deeper into the woods.

The facts surrounding the fateful voyage of November 30, 1842, unfolded as follows. The barque *Isadore* sailed down the final stretch of the Kennebec River on the ebbing tide. The day was overcast; the weather was cold; and the western sky was a foreboding shade of red as the *Isadore* majestically entered the sea for the first time on Friday afternoon. She was one man short of a full complement, though she numbered fifteen aboard, for she had taken on a passenger. The flag on her mast lay flat and still, the wind so light the ship could barely make steerage. It was the fabled calm before the storm.

The somber crowd on the shore stood in the cold, watching the ship depart with a mixture of apprehension and excitement. The normal cheerful farewells and good wishes were noticeably absent. Several women sobbed as they waved goodbye to their kinfolk. Others were watching a curious little cloud swoop in from the north, just below the heavy bank massing above. The cloud moved rapidly across the water and met the *Isadore* a half-mile offshore. It dropped a brief snow squall on the ship before continuing its journey south. As the snow dissipated, an errant ray of sunshine turned the flakes swirling around the distant barque an eerie blood-red color. Moments later, the squall was gone and the unusual calm had returned.

The *Isadore* stayed in sight of the coast for several hours, moving at a slow four knots on her southbound course. As darkness fell, the temperature dropped rapidly. Fear clutched the hearts of the townsfolk, for the barometer was predicting a storm.

As a forty-knot nor'easter roared down upon the Maine coast, the *Isadore* was eclipsed by heavy snow falling horizontally in the howling winds. Massive waves lifted her in their grip and slammed her back down into the watery canyons that separated them. Ice made the lines and decks dangerously slick. The captain gave orders to sail closer to shore, hoping to find a safe haven to ride out the storm. But the ship was cast against the treacherous rocks of Bald Head Cliff and battered to pieces by the storm surge. Amidst the tumult, all fifteen hands were lost.

A fisherman saw the first pieces of wreckage wash ashore at dawn amidst a foot of snow. He summoned help, and people collected rapidly along the coast, hoping to rescue some of the crew. But there was no one left to save. When enough pieces were gathered, they identified the wreck as the *Isadore*. Over the next several days, seven bodies were washed ashore to fill the seven caskets seen in the prophetic dream.

When I heard about the wreck, I emerged from hiding and offered to return the advanced wages the captain had given me. But the captain's business partners were so relieved when they learned one of their seamen had survived the *Isadore* disaster that they told me to keep the money.

Many townsfolk were not happy to see me when I returned to Kennebunk, especially those who lost kin. They forgave me once my story was told, but I still felt uncomfortable living among them as the lone survivor of the *Isadore*. I discussed matters with the missus, and we decided to pack up house and move to New Hampshire. The Good Lord had given us a second chance, and we should take it. Time to start over.

Ten Dollars

FORT KENT

Mon Dieu! There is no more stubborn man on earth than your grandfather! *He* says he has a strong will. I tell you, *ma petite*, that he is just plain stubborn and always has been, which is how he came to have trouble with a *loup-garou.*

Now the *loup-garou* are men just like anybody else, until they get themselves into some kind of mischief, which makes them susceptible to the workings of the devil. Once the devil has gotten them in his clutches, he transforms them into wolves and makes them do his work. Mostly this happens to those misguided souls who neglect their religious duties and do not help the poor. But sometimes a man will become a *loup-garou* because he dies without having settled his outstanding debts, and this bars him from heaven until the creditor forgives the debt before God.

Now it happened many years ago that Henri, an old friend of ours, died while still owing your grandfather ten dollars. This may not seem such a large debt to you children, but back in 1885, ten dollars was a full week's pay. Your grandfather was quite angry with our friend. He swore an oath, saying he would not forgive old Henri his debt even though it meant that his

TEN DOLLARS

bon ami's soul would never get into heaven. I chided your grandfather for his uncharitable sentiment, but he was stubborn and refused to consider it.

"*Mais non*," he shouted at me. "I will not forgive this debt, not even if Henri himself should come back from the grave and beg for my charity."

These were foolish words, and so I told your grandfather. But once his mind was made up, he would no more give in to me than he would to any man or woman. As I said before, he is the most stubborn man *le bon Dieu* ever created.

In truth, I suspected that your grandfather missed his *bon ami* and was hoping his stubborn vow would summon Henri's ghost, so that he could see his friend one more time. Whatever the reason, Grandfather stayed awake night after night, peering out the window or sitting grimly by the fire until sunrise. But Henri did not materialize, which made your grandfather very cranky indeed.

One winter night, your grandfather was out late buying supplies. He hitched our horse to the sleigh right about sunset and started for home through the woods. The moon was full, and it gleamed brightly off the snow as Grandfather drove home. Grandfather noticed a shadow slipping in and out of the trees, following the sleigh. When it glided through a patch of moonlight, he saw it was a large wolf. The wolf's eyes glowed with an uncanny light that made your grandfather's skin crawl with fear. Its feet barely touched the ground as it raced through the deep snow.

Grandfather grabbed his whip and urged the horse into a gallop. The horse was terrified by the large, stealthy creature that was following them and gladly ran when bidden. The strange wolf easily kept up with the speeding sleigh. Fearing that he would founder his horse if he kept up such a terrible pace in such cold weather, Grandfather slowed the trembling horse to a walk, watching the wolf as he did so. Immediately, the wolf slowed down until it was walking beside the sleigh. Grandfather looked down at the strange wolf, and it looked back at him with its strange, glowing eyes. At that moment Grandfather realized that the creature was a *loup-garou*.

Then the creature spoke: "*Mon ami,* you must forgive my debt. Release me from the ten dollars I owe you." With a start, Grandfather realized that the *loup-garou* was Henri. He had come at last to ask him to cancel the debt. Now Grandfather might have forgiven Henri despite his oath to the contrary if Henri had apologized or displayed deep sorrow over his debt. Your grandfather has a soft spot for people in need. But the *loup-garou* who had once been Henri did not appear repentant to your grandfather. He sounded arrogant and demanding, and that made your grandfather angry.

"I will not forgive your debt," Grandfather shouted at the *loup-garou*. "You can go to blazes!"

Grandfather urged his horse into a trot and drove briskly homeward, ignoring the *loup-garou* pacing beside him. As they reached the edge of the woods, the *loup-garou* said, "Release me from the ten dollars I owe you."

"No!" shouted Grandfather, whipping his horse to a gallop. The poor horse was trembling with fear and exhaustion, but it obeyed his command, and the sleigh flew over the moonlit snow. The *loup-garou* flew beside it. As they drew near to the house, the *loup-garou* cried again, "Release me from the ten dollars I owe you!" Once again, your grandfather refused to forgive his debt.

Grandfather pulled up in front of the barn and unhitched his poor horse, which had grown resigned to its fate and stood still despite the presence of the huge wolf sitting beside the barn door. The *loup-garou* watched every move your grandfather made with its huge, glowing eyes.

"*Mon ami*, you must forgive my debt," the *loup-garou* said softly. "Release me from the ten dollars I owe you."

"I will not forgive your debt," said Grandfather stubbornly. "You can go to blazes!"

Grandfather led the terrified horse into the barn, and the *loup-garou* followed them inside and leaped into a manger. Grandfather put the horse into a stall at the far end of the barn and walked back to where the *loup-garou* crouched in the hay. For a long moment, your very stubborn grandfather and the very stubborn *loup-garou* stood eye-to-eye and glared at one another. Then your foolish grandfather gave a snort of disgust, turned his back to the *loup-garou*, and walked toward the barn door. That's when the wolf struck. It leapt from the manger, knocking your grandfather to the floor of the barn, and its teeth closed on your grandfather's neck, though it did not break his skin.

"Release me from the ten dollars I owe you," growled the *loup-garou*.

Your grandfather was terrified. He was sure the *loup-garou* meant to kill him. Suddenly, his stubborn pride broke and he cried, "I release you from your ten dollars. Now go to blazes and leave me in peace!"

At his words, the *loup-garou* vanished in a flash of light. Trembling with fear and anger, Grandfather stood up and marched out of the barn. His rage carried him halfway across the yard before it petered out. He stopped suddenly and looked up into the starry sky, realizing he had just lost his chance to say a proper goodbye to his *bon ami*. His mouth twisted in pain and tears filled his eyes. "Henri," he said huskily. "I'm sorry."

Grandfather's words were softly spoken, but they were enough. A large wolf emerged from the edge of the woods. Small lights gathered around its body, twisting and turning in a dizzying motion until they eclipsed the beast, and then a man stood in its place. Henri looked your grandfather in the eye and nodded.

"Walk with God, *mon ami*," Grandfather said softly, pulling out his handkerchief and wiping his eyes. "Until we meet again."

Henri smiled and held up his hand in farewell. There was already a hint of paradise in his face when he disappeared.

Grandfather entered the house and stalked over to the chair where I sat mending his socks. I didn't know then what had happened to him, but I could see he was in a tizzy about something. "I hope you are satisfied!" he said to me. "I have forgiven Henri his debt. But not until his *loup-garou* had me by the neck!"

He showed me his collar, which was ripped in half from the wolf's teeth. When I saw his neck, which was covered with white froth from the creature's mouth, I gasped in horror and leapt to my feet. I hurried to the kitchen to grab a water basin and a towel, but something unexpected caught my eye and I slid to a halt beside the kitchen table.

"Pierre, where did this money come from?" I asked.

Grandfather looked at me in surprise. "What money?" he asked. Then he saw the ten-dollar bill sitting in the center of the table and sat down abruptly in the chair I had just vacated. He started shaking, and large tears rolled down his worn cheeks.

"It came from H . . . Henri," he said at last, his voice trembling with emotion. "It came from *mon ami*."

After that your grandfather was never quite as stubborn. But it took a *loup-garou* to soften him.

Logging

BUCKFIELD

I spent summers working on my parents' farm but come winter I liked to earn extra cash as a teamster at the logging camps that were so prevalent in the north woods of Maine. So, I packed up my team, and we went over to the camp on Streaked Mountain late one fall to see if they could use some help hauling logs from point A to point B. I had the job almost as soon as I opened my mouth. Nice and easy!

The camp boss was a regular "Paul Bunyan" type. Must have been descended from that legendary logger, because he really knew his stuff. As soon as I saw the tote road they carved from the logging site to the drop zone, I knew we were in for a good season. It was perfectly engineered, level in most places with a very slight downhill grade in others. Not too steep, mind, or you'd get a runaway timber sled, and that can really mess you up.

You can haul huge loads of timber on an ice-covered tote road. Easy-peasy. I should know. I've become an expert over the last few years. The logging sleds I drove had twelve-foot cross-wood bunks mounted on top. The lumbermen piled the logs eight feet high, sometimes more, and each load weighed tens of

LOGGING

tons. Not a problem on the ice-slicked Streaked Mountain tote road, but I wouldn't try it with a wagon in springtime mud.

After hauling timber all day, I was happy to get back to camp, tend my horses, and gossip with some of my buddies around the fire. Nobody tells better stories than a lumberman, except maybe the sailors over on the coast. Storytelling and cards became our favorite evening activities. Tall tales and jokes were predominant, but I loved the supernatural stories best. I was teased about my love of the unseen world, but my buddies indulged me with at least one ghost story a week.

A couple of fellows who just joined our crew told a hair-raising tale that occurred to them on their journey north. The two lumbermen stopped one evening in a small town and asked if there was a free place where they could camp. They were directed to an abandoned cabin just outside the village limits but warned that it was haunted. According to villagers, the family who lived there once took in a handsome young man as a boarder. He fell in love with the daughter of the house, and asked her to marry him, but before they were wed, he was murdered by a jealous rival. His betrothed died shortly thereafter of a broken heart, and her spirit still haunted the house, looking for her beloved. The two lumbermen weren't afraid of ghosts, so they set up camp in the creaky old structure. They were fast asleep when a cold breeze came swirling through the front chamber, banging the shutters and rattling every window. The men jerked awake and saw the glowing form of a young woman floating through the room, searching for something . . . or someone. She passed their makeshift beds and drifted into the next room, and the one after. The phantom light slowly faded as she wafted through the kitchen and out the back door. When the light vanished, the lumbermen fell back into their bedding, gasping in shock. "Next time, I'm paying for a room at the inn," one of the fellows said. His buddy agreed.

Their story made me shiver, so I moved closer to the fire. I was sure glad nothing was haunting me. I didn't know what I'd do if I saw a ghost. Cry like a baby, probably, which would be embarrassing.

I thought about the ghost story as I drove the heavy timber sled down the tote road the next morning. That poor young ghost was doomed to search for her love as the house withered and died around her. I sighed at the thought and then frowned when I saw a man's tall figure ambling down the tote road ahead of me. Nobody I knew, as far as I could tell from that distance. And not friendly, or he'd have hailed me. The fellow was probably taking a shortcut, I decided, although where he was going, I couldn't reckon. Our lumber camp was the only settlement in the area. He must be a hermit living in the back of beyond, not unheard of in these parts. I shrugged, curiosity satisfied. I returned to my occult musings, and when next I looked, the fellow was gone.

The next supernatural story came a few evenings later, and it was even better than the first. A logger named Pierre told us his favorite spooky story, which quickly became mine as well. It seemed a lumberman near the Canadian border was more fond of lounging, lunchtime, and ladies than he was of timber, so he made a deal with the devil. In exchange for his soul, the devil would give him a magic axe that would work without ceasing whenever he whistled a tune. The axe would cut timber better than any logger, and the lumberman lounged in the shade, whistling while the axe worked. He made a lot of money with his magic axe, and he spent it in the local saloons, where he courted the ladies, picked fights, and ate until he was fit to burst. But his debauchery finally caught up with him. His whistles weren't so merry as his health declined, and the magic axe became more menacing than helpful. The lumberman started wondering what happened in the afterlife when a man sold his soul to the devil. Probably nothing good. He decided he should go and confess his sins to the local priest, but he never made it out of the camp. The next morning when the loggers went to the work site, the lumberman's body was found in the woods. His head had been chopped off by the magic axe, which was never seen again.

I told the story of the magic axe to the loggers who loaded up my timber sled the next morning. They laughed with delight and said it might be worth it to own such an axe. I was still chuckling as I drove the team onto the tote road. Nearing the bend, I saw the tall man appear suddenly in the middle of the road ahead. I blinked in surprise. One minute the way was clear, the next he was there, drifting toward the curve. What a strange fellow. He was gone by the time I reached the spot, and I couldn't see any footprints on the packed snow and the ice.

Between card games and tall tales, I had lots to think about as I drove back and forth along the tote road every day, with only my horses for company along the way. Unless you counted the mysterious hermit who took the shortcut along the tote road at the same time each day. He was always out of earshot of the lumber sled, and he never paused to say hello. He just drifted ahead of me to the bend in the road and vanished. Must be shy.

We'd been in camp a month, and I was still racking my brain, trying to figure out a good ghost story to tell my friends. All the tales from my hometown could be summed up in a single sentence: "I saw something spooky and I ran like a baby." Not a compelling tale.

Fortunately for me, a farmer from the coast had a doozy of a story that night. A few years back, he was working at a lumber camp not far from here when a howling blizzard stopped work for a couple of days. A stranger stumbled into the camp on the second day, exhausted and nearly frozen to death. The lumbermen warmed him up by the fire and the camp cook filled him with good food. When he recovered, he showed them many magic tricks to help pass the time until the storm was over. No one could figure out how he made objects disappear into thin air or pulled them out of nothing. They decided he must be a conjuror from one of the traveling shows, looking for winter work. The stranger proved to be as good a lumberman as he was a magician. He could fell trees with the best of them, and even remove trees that were lodged, something only the best of the best could manage. One evening, another big snowstorm blew in. When it cleared the next morning, the stranger was gone. The only thing he left behind was a set of cloven footprints leading away from camp. The devil had been among them!

As we loaded the last of the logs onto my sled the next morning, Pierre came over and said: "*Mon ami*, I have been meaning to ask you. Have you seen anything of the headless ghost that haunts this mountain?"

"The what now?" I asked, startled.

"A friend warned me about the headless ghost when he learned I intended to seek work in this lumber camp. A man was decapitated in a lumbering accident near here, and his spirit is said to roam the lower slopes of the Streaked Mountain, bound forever to the place where he lost his head. You have traveled these roads more than the rest of us. I thought perhaps you might have seen this wonder."

"Not a glimpse," I assured him.

Pierre seemed disappointed. "Maybe one day," he said, as if to comfort me for this loss.

"I hope not," I muttered as I climbed up onto the piled wood. I started my team, and waved farewell to Pierre.

As I navigated out of the work site and onto the tote road, I pondered this story. They had been lumbering parts of the Streaked Mountain for several years now, and accidents always happened, even when you had a "Paul Bunyan" for a boss. Perhaps a logger had lost his head somewhere on this mountain. How sad.

Ahead of me, I saw the tall hermit taking his short cut along the tote road. He was closer to me this time, almost within hailing distance. As I watched him drift slowly toward the curve in the road, I suddenly realized the man wasn't making any footprints in the new fallen snow. I blinked several times, unable to believe my eyes. Then I realized his feet were floating several inches above the snow and he had no head! There was only a bloody stump above his broad shoulders.

No, wait, I was wrong. He did have a head. It was firmly tucked underneath his arm.

When he heard my strangled yell, the man did a funny floating turn and lifted his head above the bloody stump of his neck so he could look at me. I screamed. This spooked the horses, and they reared in their traces wanting to run. I pulled them to a halt before the sled slid off the tote road, then fumbled for my rifle. I fired at the ghastly figure floating toward me, and the bullet came whizzing back over my head as if it had bounced off an invisible wall. When I raised my gun for a second shot, the rifle barrel began twisting until it was pointed straight back at me. I dropped it onto the piled-up timber with a gasp and stared at the phantom, my eyes like saucers. I had no idea what to do.

The horses were jittering in their harness. If they tried to run again, it could easily prove fatal. The phantom laughed wickedly, amused by my predicament. Then he drifted toward the curve and his body sank into the icy ground. His severed head lingered above the road for a moment, leering at me. Then it too descended into the ice.

I flopped back onto the timber, my heart pounding so hard my chest hurt. "Don't spook the horses. Don't spook the horses." I kept muttering this refrain to myself until my pulse evened out. I was panic sweating all over, and I couldn't stop shaking. My trembling fingers couldn't close around the reins, so I clicked my tongue to get the horses moving again. We paused at the spot where the phantom descended into the road. Maybe this was the place where he died? There was no way to tell.

I was much calmer by the time evening rolled around. Tonight, it was my turn to tell a ghost story, and it was a good one. When I finished the tale, everyone laughed as if I had told them a joke. "It's true, I swear," I said, miffed that my buddies didn't believe me. "I saw a headless ghost on the tote road this morning."

They laughed even harder than before, except for Pierre. The tall lumberman motioned them to silence and stood up. "I believe you, *mon ami*," he said, giving me a mocking bow. Then he removed his head and tucked it under his arm. My mouth dropped open in shock when I realized he was the tall ghost who had been haunting me on the tote road.

Conversation ceased abruptly all over the room. Every eye was on Pierre as he lifted his severed head above the bloody stump of his neck. He turned it slowly so he could look at the assembled lumbermen, and we could look at him. Then Pierre laughed, long and loud, just as he had on the tote road. The wicked glee in his voice made every hair on my body stand on end.

Pierre stretched out one arm, and a glowing axe flew through the door and slapped into his hand. I gaped at it, all the puzzle pieces fitting together in my mind. This must be the magic axe from Pierre's spooky tale. Which meant . . . oh good lord . . . that he was the lumberman who sold his soul to the devil!

As if he had heard my thoughts, Pierre turned toward me with an evil grin. He made another mocking bow, and then his body sank through the floor until only his severed head remained visible.

"Don't spook the horses," he said wickedly, winking at me.

Then his head vanished through the floorboards with a faint "pop."

Tables and chairs tumbled every which way as loggers fled the room. On my way to the door, I stumbled over a big lumberjack who had fainted from fright. Grabbing him under the arms, I dragged him outside with the rest of us.

By noon next day, the camp at Streaked Mountain had officially closed for the season. I was the first person in line to claim my pay. Money secured, I hitched my team to a cutter and made a swift exit, headed for home. I'd need to find another way to make money next winter. Logging was obviously not for me!

Resources

Allen, Chandler Briggs. "Wreck of the Bark Isadore Most Shocking Tragedy Ever Enacted on Maine Coast." *Portland (ME) Sunday Telegram*, April 13, 1924.

"Anecdotes. The Barber's Ghost." *Shasta (CA) Courier*, September 6, 1873.

Arduinna (2000). *La Chasse Gallerie.* www.ygora.net/nav/page_index/contes/contes/obscur/obscur_27.htm (accessed August 24, 2004).

Asfar, Dan, and Edrick Thay. *Ghost Stories of America.* Edmonton, AB: Ghost House Books, 2001.

"Away Down East." *Ellsworth (ME) American*, September 23, 1886.

"The Barber's Ghost." *Eastport (ME) Sentinel*, January 29, 1825.

"The Barber's Ghost: A Fact." *Independent Statesman* (Portland, ME), November 19, 1824.

Beck, Horace P. *The Folklore of Maine.* Philadelphia: J. B. Lippincott, 1957.

Bolt, Mary. *Haunted New England: A Devilish View of the Yankee Past.* New York: Weathervane Books, 1972.

Botkin, B. A. *A Treasury of American Folklore.* New York: Crown, 1944.

Botkin, B. A., ed. *A Treasury of New England Folklore.* New York: Crown, 1965.

Bruchac, Joseph, and James Bruchac. *When the Chenoo Howls: Native American Tales of Terror.* New York: Walker, 1998.

Burby, Tom. "The Phantom Trains of the North Woods." Strange New England podcast, July 23, 2022. https://strangenewengland.com/podcast/the-phantom-trains-of-the-north-woods/.

Burns, Adam. *Maine Railroads: State Map, History, Abandoned Lines.* American-Rails.com, September 7, 2024. https://www.american-rails.com/me.html.

Citro, Joseph A. *Weird New England.* New York: Sterling, 2005.

Costopoulos, Nina. *Lighthouse Ghosts and Legends.* Birmingham, AL: Crane Hill Publishers, 2003.

Cummin, Sharon. "Captain Leander Foss and His Shipwrecks." Kennebunkport Historical Society, November 26, 2021. https://kporths.com/2021/11/26/captain-leander-foss-and-his-shipwrecks/.

"The Dead Ship of Harpswell." New England Legends podcast, January 11, 2024. https://ournewenglandlegends.com/podcast-331-the-dead-ship-of-harpswell/#transcript.

Downer, Deborah L. *Classic American Ghost Stories.* Little Rock, AR: August House Publishers, 1990.

Drake, Samuel Adams. *A Book of New England Legends and Folk Lore.* Boston: Little, Brown, 1883.

Dunwich, Gerina. *A Witch's Halloween.* Avon, MA: Provenance Press, 2007.

———. *The Pagan Book of Halloween.* New York: Penguin Group, 2000.

Emery-Waterhouse, Frances. "Sailor's Strange Dream Foretold Famous Maine Shipwreck." *Sun Journal* (Lewiston, ME), March 19, 1966.

"Explore Several Unique, Off-the-Beat-Path Destinations in Maine: Jasper Beach." *Bangor (ME) Daily News,* June 21, 2012.

"The Fire Test. How the Spiritualists Were Regaled at an Eastern Maine Séance." *Sun Journal* (Lewiston, ME), October 5, 1895.

"Frank Baxter." *Republican Journal* (Belfast, ME), September 10, 1891.

Freeburg, Jessica, and Natalie Fowler. *Monsters of the Northeast.* Cambridge, MN: Adventure Publications, 2024.

"Ghost in Maine Beats All By an Ectoplasmic Sight." *New York Herald,* July 29, 1922.

"Ghost in Maine Just Beats All." *Lexington (KY) Herald-Leader*, August 6, 1922.

"The Ghost of a Cough or Cough of a Ghost." *Sun Journal* (Lewiston, ME), December 16, 1893.

"Giant 'Specter Moose' Reappears in Maine, Lengthening Lore of Forest Begun in 1901." *New York Times*, January 9, 1938.

Hauck, Dennis William. *Haunted Places: The National Directory*. New York: Penguin Books, 1994.

Hegeman, Geraldine, Dolores Daigle, and Marilyn Daigle. Maine / Maritimes Folklore Collection, Accession No. 179. Fall 1962. https://library.umaine.edu/content/NAFOH/text/NA0179.pdf.

"Her Spook Protector. The Ghost Upset Prospective Maine Matrimony and Unmasked a Villain." *Cleveland Plain Dealer*, January 1, 1894.

Ives, Edward D. "Malecite and Passamaquoddy Tales." *Northeast Folklore*, Vol. 6, 1964.

Johnson, Blair. "Harpswell Tales Make Your Blood Run Cold." *Times Record* (Brunswick, ME), October 29, 1979.

Johnson, Clifton. *New England and Its Neighbors*. New York: Macmillan, 1902.

Jones, Louis C. *Things That Go Bump in the Night*. New York: Hill and Wang, 1959.

Juettner, Carie. *Ghostly Tales of New England*. Charleston, SC: Arcadia Children's Books, 2020.

"The Late Storm." *Washingtonian Journal* (Portland, ME), December 7, 1842.

Latimer, Greg. *Ghosts of the Boothbay Region*. Charleston, SC: Haunted America, 2015.

______. *Pirates and Lost Treasure of Coastal Maine*. Charleston, SC: Haunted America, 2020.

Le Blanc, Charles. *Contes et Légendes du Quebec*. Paris: Nathan, 1999.

LeBeau, Julie. *La Chasse-Galerie*. elfwood.lysator.liu.se/art/j/u/juliel/chasse.jpg.html (accessed August 24, 2004).

LiBrizzi, Marcus. *Dark Woods, Chill Waters: Ghost Tales from Down East Maine*. Camden, ME: Down East Books, 2007.

______. *Ghosts of Acadia*. Camden, ME: Down East Books, 2011.

______. *Haunted Islands in the Gulf of Maine*. Guilford, CT: Down East Books, 2017.

LiBrizzi, Marcus, ed. *The Nelly Butler Hauntings*. Machias, ME: Library of Early Maine Literature, University of Maine at Machias, 2010.

"Maine's Spectre Moose Again." *Sun* (New York, NY), September 23, 1900.

Marrow, Adam. *Pirate Ghosts & Buried Treasures of the Northeast Coast: A Historical Assessment on Pirate Folklore*. Middletown, DE: Picaroon Press, 2024.

McCormick, Dell J. *Paul Bunyan Swings His Axe*. Caldwell, ID: Caxton Printers, 1936.

Mead, Alice, and Arnold Neptune. *Giants of the Dawnland*. South Portland, ME: Loose Cannon Press, 2015.

"Mediator Brown Dies at 87 Years. Hermit of Boarstone Mountain Is No More." *Sun Journal* (Lewiston, ME), June 10, 1912.

"The Mediator of Maine. Death of Character Who Claimed to Act as Intermediary Between God and Man." *Washington Post*, July 7, 1912.

Monroe, Judith W. *Peripheral Visions*. Durham, NC: Crones' Own Press, 1992.

Mueller, Mickie. *Llewellyn's Little Book of Halloween*. Woodbury, MN: Llewellyn Publications, 2018.

NA 005, manuscript, 1962, Text: NA 0054. *Hunting, Trapping, Poaching, and Recreational Fishing*. MF181. Northeast Archives of Folklore and Oral History. https://archives.library.umaine.edu/repositiories/5/arhival_objects/356732 (accessed September 16, 2025).

NA 0061, manuscript, 1963, Text: NA 0061. *Hunting, Trapping, Poaching and Recreational Fishing*. MF181. Northeast Archives of Folklore and Oral History.

NA 0062, manuscript, 1963, Text: NA 0062. *Hunting, Trapping, Poaching, and Recreational Fishing*. MF181. Northeast Archives of Folklore and Oral History. https://archives.library.umaine.edu/

repositories/5/archival_objects/356768 (accessed October 6, 2025).

NA 0179, manuscript, Fall 1962, Audio: NA 0179. *Woods Music Collection*. MF180. Northeast Archives of Folklore and Oral History. https://archives.library.umaine.edu/repositories/5/archival_objects/347725 (accessed September 13, 2025).

NA 0280, manuscript, 1962, Text: NA 0280. *Hunting, Trapping, Poaching, and Recreational Fishing*. MF181. Northeast Archives of Folklore and Oral History. https://archives.library.umaine.edu/repositories/5/archival_objects/356837 (accessed October 6, 2025).

NA 0341, manuscript, May 12, 1962, Text: NA 0341. *Hunting, Trapping, Poaching, and Recreational Fishing*. MF181. Northeast Archives of Folklore and Oral History. https://archives.library.umaine.edu/repositories/5/archival_objects/356859 (accessed October 6, 2025).

NA 0552, transcript, 1970, Audio: NA 0552. *Lumberman's Life Series*, MF012. Northeast Archives of Folklore and Oral History. https://archives.library.umaine.edu/repositories/5/archival_objects/325142 (accessed October 6, 2025).

NA 1438, text, December 15, 1980, Text: NA 1438. *Bowdoin College Folklore Papers*. MF006. Northeast Archives of Folklore and Oral History. https://library.umaine.edu/content/NAFOH/text/NA 1438.pdf.

Nason, Emma Huntington. *Old Hallowell on the Kennebec*. Augusta, ME: Loudon Hill, 1909.

"Newark Residents See Ghost in Maine." *Daily Record* (Long Branch, NJ), July 28, 1922.

Noel, Lynn. *La Chasse-Galerie*, 1989. homepage.mac.com/lynnoel/pubs/Chasse-Galerie.pdf (accessed August 24, 2004).

Norman, Michael, and Beth Scott. *Historic Haunted America*. New York: Tor Books, 1995.

Packard, Christopher. *Mythical Creatures of Maine*. Camden, ME: Down East Books, 2021.

"The Phantom Schooner. The Weird Helmsman Off Schooner Head, Mt. Desert." *Portland (ME) Daily Press*, August 11, 1885.

"The Phantom Train." *New York Times*, May 16, 1886.

"Phantom Trains." Strange New England podcast. YouTube, 2022. https://youtu.be/OQ4SO-lWN_Q?si=GGAFQkbLz6ib6kdo.

Piper, Hank. "Portland's Famous Ghost Stories." *Portland*, Fall 1985.

Plumb, Taryn. *Haunted Maine Lighthouses.* Camden, ME: Down East Books, 2018.

Reevy, Tony. *Ghost Train!* Lynchburg, VA: TLC Publishing, 1998.

Rusk, Tobin. *Haunted Places in Maine.* Middletown, DE: Independently published, 2025.

Schlosser, S. E. Field interview, Machiasport resident "R.A." September 7, 2025.

"Schooner Head. A Legend of the Days of Captain Kidd." *Carrollton (MO) Daily Democrat*, September 16, 1885.

Schulte, Carol Olivieri. *Ghosts on the Coast of Maine.* Camden, ME: Down East Books, 1989.

Seavey, Wendell. *Working the Sea.* Berkeley, CA: North Atlantic Books, 2005.

Shea, Mrs. James (Estelle), interviewed by David Currier. *Lumberman's Life Series*, MF012. Northeast Archives of Folklore and Oral History.

Simpson, Dorothy. *The Maine Islands in Story and Legend.* Philadelphia: J. B. Lippincott, 1960.

Skelton, Kathryn. "Weird, Wicked Weird: The Ghost Moose That Got Away." *Sun Journal* (Lewiston, ME), June 21, 2019.

Skinner, Charles M. *American Myths and Legends.* Vol. 1. Philadelphia: J. B. Lippincott, 1903.

_______. *Myths and Legends of Our Own Land.* Vols. 1 and 2. Philadelphia: J. B. Lippincott, 1896.

Smitten, Susan. *Ghost Stories of New England.* Auburn, WA: Ghost House Books, 2003.

Souliere, Michelle W. *Strange Maine: True Tales from the Pine Tree State.* Charleston, SC: History Press, 2010.

"'Specter Moose' in Maine's Woods." *Montana Record-Herald* (Helena, MT), October 7, 1900.

"Specter Moose Is Maine Sensation." *Call-Leader* (Elwood, IN), February 21, 1938.

"A Specter Moose of Maine Woods." *Evening World-Herald* (Omaha, NE), November 27, 1908.

"Spiritual Phenomena." *Portland (ME) Daily Press*, July 10, 1874.

Stansfield Jr., Charles A. *Haunted Maine.* Mechanicsburg, PA: Stackpole Books, 2007.

"State Chat." *Sun Journal* (Lewiston, ME), January 20, 1896.

"A State of Maine Ghost." *Minneapolis Journal*, July 10, 1912.

Sylvester, Herbert Milton. *Maine Pioneer Settlements: Old York.* Boston: W. B. Clarke, 1909.

Thaxter, Celia. *Among the Isles of Shoals.* Boston: Office of the Librarian of Congress at Washington, DC, 1909.

"A Thumping Big Moose." *Daily Kennebec Journal* (Augusta, ME), October 20, 1900.

Titcomb, Frances Emery. "Restoration of Monument Recalls Early Tragedy at Kennebunkport." *Portland (ME) Press Herald*, July 24, 1938.

Townsend, Amanda. "Road Trip Worthy: This Beach Is Covered in Beautiful Stones But May Also Be Haunted." Q1065.com, September 20, 2017. https://q1065.fm/road-trip-worthy-this-beach-is-covered-in-beautiful-stones-but-may-also-be-haunted/.

Urban, Tony. *New England's Unexplained Mysteries.* Packanack Publishing, 2023.

Various, interviewed by Ethelyn Christie. *Hunting, Trapping, Poaching, and Recreational Fishing.* MF181. Northeast Archives of Folklore and Oral History.

Various, interviewed by Iona Coffin. *Hunting, Trapping, Poaching, and Recreational Fishing.* MF181. Northeast Archives of Folklore and Oral History.

Various, interviewed by Mabel Small. *Hunting, Trapping, Poaching, and Recreational Fishing.* MF181. Northeast Archives of Folklore and Oral History.

Various, interviewed by Nora Roach. *Hunting, Trapping, Poaching, and Recreational Fishing*. MF181. Northeast Archives of Folklore and Oral History.

Various, interviewed by Roger Mitchell and Joyce Mitchell. *Hunting, Trapping, Poaching, and Recreational Fishing*. MF181. Northeast Archives of Folklore and Oral History.

Verde, Tom. *Maine Ghosts & Legends*. Camden, ME: Down East Books, 1989.

WHAV News Staff. "Haverhill's Cursed Son, Jonathan Buck." WHAV.net: Wavelengths, October 23, 2016. https://whav.net/2016/10/23/haverhills-cursed-son-jonathan-buck.

"The Witch's Curse and the Stone Foot." *Philadelphia Inquirer*, July 17, 1898.

"With the Long Bow." *Minneapolis Journal*, March 28, 1925.

"Wreck of Isadore Recalled by Old Religious Paper." *Biddeford-Saco Journal* (Biddeford, ME), July 3, 1930.

Zwicker, Roxie J. *Haunted Portland: From Pirates to Ghost Brides*. Charleston, SC: Haunted America, 2007.

______. *Haunted York County*. Charleston, SC: Haunted America, 2010.

______. *Maine Book of the Dead: Graveyard Legends and Lore*. Charleston, SC: History Press, 2021.

About the Author

S. E. Schlosser has been telling stories since she was a child, when games of "let's pretend" quickly built themselves into full-length tales acted out with friends. A graduate of Houghton College, the Institute of Children's Literature, and Rutgers University, she created and maintains the award-winning website Americanfolklore.net, where she shares a wealth of stories from all fifty states, some dating back to the origins of America. Sandy spends much of her time answering questions from visitors to the site. Many of her favorite emails come from other folklorists who delight in practicing the old tradition of "who can tell the tallest tale."

About the Illustrator

Artist **Paul Hoffman** trained in painting and printmaking, with his first extensive illustration work on assignment in Egypt, drawing ancient wall reliefs for the University of Chicago. His work graces books of many genres—children's titles, textbooks, short story collections, natural history volumes, and numerous textbooks. For *Spooky Maine*, he employed a scratchboard technique and an active imagination.

www.ingramcontent.com/pod-product-compliance
Lightning Source LLC
LaVergne TN
LVHW090333100626
840870LV00032B/384